THE BEST OF
Jane Austen
KNITS

27 Regency-Inspired Designs

Edited by
AMY CLARKE MOORE

INTERWEAVE
interweave.com

EDITOR Michelle Bredeson

TECHNICAL EDITORS
Tracey Davidson, Karen Frisa,
Lori Gayle, Kristen TenDyke

FACT-CHECKERS Sheryl Craig,
Susan Forgue

ASSOCIATE ART DIRECTOR
Charlene Tiedemann

DESIGN Brenda Gallagher

LAYOUT & PRODUCTION
Katherine Jackson

PHOTOGRAPHERS Ann Sabin Swanson,
Christa Tippmann

Interweave
A division of F+W Media, Inc.
4868 Innovation Drive
Fort Collins, CO 80525
interweave.com

Manufactured in China by
RR Donnelley Shenzhen.

Library of Congress
Cataloging-in-Publication Data

The best of Jane Austen knits : 27 re-
gency-inspired designs / edited by Amy
Clarke Moore.
     pages cm
  Includes index.
ISBN 978-1-62033-881-0 (pbk.)
ISBN 978-1-62033-882-7 (PDF)
1. Knitting--Patterns. I. Moore, Amy
Clarke, 1969- II. Jane Austen knits.
  TT8250B3995 2014
  746.43'2--dc23

2014024297

10 9 8 7 6 5 4 3 2 1

Contents

Introduction

PHOTO: SHERYL CRAIG

Literature and knitting seem to be a perfect pairing—especially when you consider the work of Jane Austen. Perhaps this is because knitting, like reading, has a meditative, quiet quality. Jane Austen's novels resonate with knitters for the same reason they have resonated with readers around the world for centuries—Jane Austen captures the essence of humanity: quietly, succinctly, and with rich humor.

Her stories are timeless. Through them we gain insight into a world (specifically the Regency era, 1795–1837, in England) that was governed by social class and strict rules of decorum. But at the same time, Jane Austen weaves narratives about people pursuing happiness despite obstacles; remaining true to themselves while still being loyal to their family and friends; and struggling to know themselves—stories that transcend time, place, and situation.

Still, there are some who look no further than the surface of Jane Austen's novels and conclude that they are nothing more than well-written and engaging romances—enjoyable and entertaining. But if you take the time to look deeper, you will continue to find riches of social, political, and economic insight. You'll find commentary on the significant forces that were shaping our modern world at the time. Consider some of the world events that were taking place during Jane Austen's brief lifetime—1775–1817: the Industrial Revolution; the publication of Adam Smith's *The Wealth of Nations* and Mary Wollstonecraft's *The Vindication of the Rights of Women*; the American

Revolution; the French Revolution; the Napoleonic Wars; the formation of the United Kingdom; and the abolishment of slavery in the British Empire.

But what do these long-ago events have to do with our pursuit of knitting as pastime today in the twenty-first century? Consider that during Jane's lifetime, almost any cloth she came into contact with was most likely hand-spun, handwoven or handknitted, and naturally dyed. As crafters, you know how much time and energy would have been devoted daily to the hand-making of the textiles that we use and depend upon for every moment of our lives, and yet take for granted—cloth is literally disposable in our current times. We have the luxury of choosing to make specialty pieces by hand—of enjoying the process and not being stressed out by the fact if we don't finish our garment, we might just freeze. That shift occurred during Jane Austen's lifetime, and as we knit and enjoy her narratives, we can appreciate how Jane not only captured this pivotal time in our history, but helped shaped the way we understand it. ❧

—*Amy Clarke Moore*

Lady Russell Shawl

JOY GERHARDT

Lady Russell, Anne Elliot's close friend in *Persuasion,* is a proper and practical noble lady. She has only good intentions when she advises Anne to marry for wealth and status rather than love, however misguided those intentions were.

This unusually shaped shawl is a fusion of elegance and practicality. As a hybrid between a half-circle shawl and a stole, it can be easily draped over the arms.

FINISHED SIZE About 23" (58.5 cm) deep and 74" (188 cm) long.

YARN Fingering weight (#1 Super Fine) *Shown here:* Fyberspates Ethereal (60% silk, 40% cashmere; 437 yd [400 m]/3½ oz [100 g]): teal, 2 skeins.

NEEDLES Body—size 6 (4 mm): circular (cir) 32" (81.5 cm) or longer. Ruffle—size 7 (4.5 mm) cir 32" (81.5 cm) or longer. Adjust needle size if necessary to obtain the correct gauge.

NOTIONS Markers (m); stitch holders or waste yarn; tapestry needle; blocking pins.

GAUGE (not critical) 23 sts and 24 rows = 4" (10 cm) in St st on larger needles; 18 sts and 24 rows = 4" (10 cm) in patt st on smaller needles.

Notes

- Less than 2 grams of yarn remained after knitting the sample shawl—to ensure you have enough yarn to complete the project, consider purchasing an extra skein.

- Charts show right-side rows only. Work wrong-side rows as given in instructions.

- The shawl is knitted like a regular half-circle shawl until the edge of the semicircle when the majority of the stitches are bound off, and the wing stitches are placed on a holder. Each of the wings is knit back and forth separately, with short-row shaping to keep them straight. Afterward, stitches are picked up along the entire bottom edge of the shawl to form a ruffled edge.

BODY

With smaller needles, using a provisional method (see Glossary), CO 3 sts. Knit 11 rows, do not turn after last row. Rotate work and pick up and knit 5 sts down selvedge (1 st from each garter ridge), then remove waste yarn from provisional CO and place 3 sts on left-hand needle, k3—11 sts.

Next row and all WS rows: K3, purl to last 3 sts, k3.

Next RS row: (RS) K3, [yo, k1] five times, yo, k3—17 sts.

Next RS row: K3, yo, k3, yo, pm, k1, yo, k3, yo, pm, k1, yo, k3, yo, k3—23 sts.

Next RS row: Knit.

Next RS row: K3, yo, [k to m, yo, sl m, k1, yo] twice, knit to last 3 sts, yo, k3—29 sts.

Next RS row: Knit.

Rep last 4 rows 3 more times—47 sts.

Beg working Chart A as foll:

Next row: (RS) K3, [work next row of Chart A, sl m, k1] twice, work next row of Chart A, k3—6 sts inc'd.

Next row: (WS) K3, purl to last 3 sts, k3.

Rep last 2 rows 71 more times—3 rep of Chart A worked; 281 sts.

Next row: (RS) K56 sts and place them on st holder, loosely BO 169 sts, removing m as you go, knit to end—56 sts on each side of middle.

WINGS

Next row: (WS) K3, purl to end.

Short-Rows

Next short-row: (RS) Sl 1, k43, wrap next st, turn, purl to end.

Next short-row: Sl 1, k38, wrap next st, turn, purl to end.

Next short-row: Sl 1, k33, wrap next st, turn, purl to end.

Next short-row: Sl 1, k28, wrap next st, turn, purl to end.

Next short-row: Sl 1, k23, wrap next st, turn, purl to end.

Next short-row: Sl 1, k18, wrap next st, turn, purl to end.

Next short-row: Sl 1, k13, wrap next st, turn, purl to end.

Beg working Chart B as foll:

Next row: (RS) Sl 1, work Chart B over next 52 sts, k3.

Next row: (WS) K3, purl to end.

Rep last 2 rows 39 more times—5 rep of Chart B. Knit 5 rows. BO all sts.

Place 56 held sts on smaller needles. Attach yarn to work RS row.

Next row: (RS) Knit.

Short-Rows

Next short-row: (WS) Sl 1, p43, wrap next st, turn, knit to end.

Next short-row: Sl 1, p38, wrap next st, turn, knit to end.

Next short-row: Sl 1, p33, wrap next st, turn, knit to end.

Next short-row: Sl 1, p28, wrap next st, turn, knit to end.

Next short-row: Sl 1, p23, wrap next st, turn, knit to end.

Next short-row: Sl 1, p18, wrap next st, turn, knit to end.

Next short-row: Sl 1, p13, wrap next st, turn, knit to end.

Beg working Chart B as foll:

Next row: (WS) Sl 1, purl to last 3 sts, k3.

Next row: (RS) K3, work Chart B over next 52 sts, k1.

Rep last 2 rows 39 more times—5 rep of Chart B. Knit 5 rows. BO all sts.

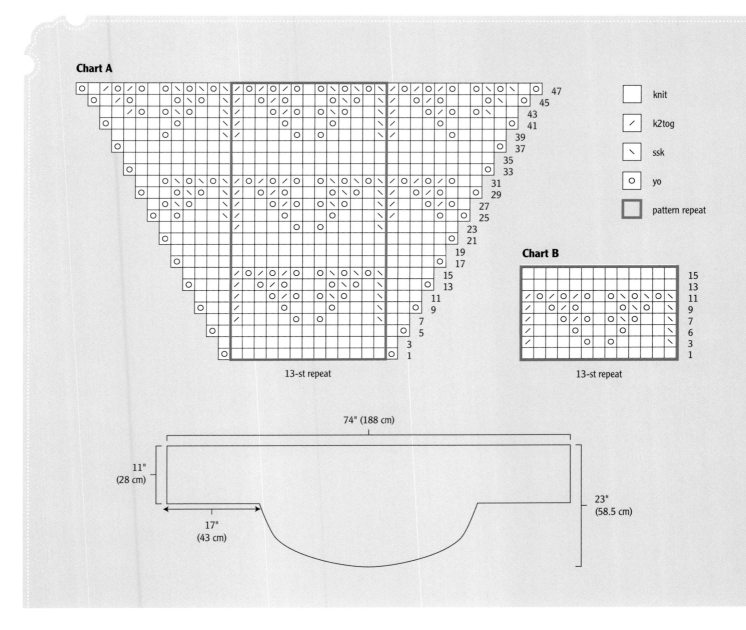

Chart A

knit

/ k2tog

\ ssk

o yo

pattern repeat

47
45
43
41
39
37
35
33
31
29
27
25
23
21
19
17
15
13
11
9
7
5
3
1

13-st repeat

Chart B

15
13
11
9
7
6
3
1

13-st repeat

74" (188 cm)

11" (28 cm)

23" (58.5 cm)

17" (43 cm)

RUFFLE

With RS facing and smaller needles, pick up and knit 76 sts along side edge of wing, place marker (pm), pick up and knit 169 sts from BO edge, pm, pick up and knit 76 sts along side of other wing—321 sts. Change to larger needles.

Next row and all WS rows: Sl 1, purl to end.

Next row: Sl 1, M1, ★[k2, M1] to 3 sts before m, k3, sl m; rep from ★ once more, k3, M1, [k2, M1] to last st, k1—478 sts.

Next RS row: Sl 1, M1, [k3, M1] to 4 sts before m, k4, sl m, [k3, M1] to 3 sts before next m, k3, sl m, k4, M1, [k3, M1] to last st, k1—635 sts.

Work in St st until ruffle measures 2" (5 cm).

BO all sts loosely.

FINISHING

Weave in all ends. To block, soak in warm water and lay flat, pinning out the lace to schematic measurements.

JOY GERHARDT is an American living in Reading, England: the town where Jane and her sister Cassandra attended school. Joy loves working with unusual yet practical shapes and seamless constructions. She documents her knitting adventures at blog.joyuna.com.

Austen Spencer

VICKI SQUARE

Around 1790, Lord Spencer got the tails of his riding jacket caught and torn off as he dismounted his horse, creating an instant fashion movement, so the story goes. The waist-length, close-fitted jacket became widely popular for gentlemen hunters and riders. Vicki Square was inspired to capture the flavor of the style with midriff length, long, slim sleeves and a low square neckline. The variations in the hand-dyed wool yarn and the stitch texture of the bodice present a Spencer with rich depth of character.

FINISHED SIZE 33 (34¾, 37, 39, 40½, 42¾, 44)" (84 [88.5, 94, 99, 103, 108.5, 112] cm) chest circumference, buttoned, including ¾" (2 cm) front band. Top shown measures 33" (84 cm).

YARN Sportweight (#2 Fine)
Shown here: Madelinetosh Tosh Sport (100% superwash Merino; 270 yd [246 m]/4¼ oz [120 g]): gilded, 4 (4, 5, 5, 5, 5, 6) skeins.

NEEDLES Size 5 (3.75 mm): 24" (60 cm) circular (cir). Adjust needle size if necessary to obtain the correct gauge.

NOTIONS Stitch markers (m); scrap yarn for stitch holders; tapestry needle; spare cir needle in same size or slightly smaller than main needle for three-needle bind-off; size F/5 (3.75 mm) crochet hook; five ½" (1.3) shank buttons.

GAUGE 21 sts and 28 rows = 4" (10 cm) in St st; 22 sts and 34 rows = 4" (10 cm) in patt from Basketweave chart.

Notes

◆ *The chart pattern is deliberately not mirrored at the side seams and does not match at the shoulder seams.*

◆ *The second stitch of a k1f&b increase produces a "bar" on the right side of the fabric. In order for the bar to appear 1 stitch in from each selvedge, the sleeve increases are worked in the first stitch at the beginning of the row, and in the second-to-last stitch at the end of the row.*

BACK

Using the long-tail method, CO 90 (96, 100, 106, 112, 118, 122) sts. Beg and ending where indicated for your size, work in patt from Basketweave chart until piece measures 5 (5, 5½, 5½, 6, 6, 6)" (12.5 [12.5, 14, 14, 15, 15, 15] cm) from CO, ending with a WS row.

Shape Armholes

Maintaining established patt, BO 5 (5, 5, 6, 7, 8, 8) sts at beg of next 2 rows—80 (86, 90, 94, 98, 102, 106) sts.

Dec row: (RS) Ssk, work in established patt to last 2 sts, k2tog—2 sts dec'd.

[Work 1 WS row even, then rep the dec row] 3 (3, 3, 4, 5, 6, 7) times—72 (78, 82, 84, 86, 88, 90) sts. Work even in patt until armholes measure 7½ (7½, 8, 8, 8½, 8½, 9)" (19 [19, 20.5, 20.5, 21.5, 21.5, 23] cm), ending with a WS row. Place all sts on scrap yarn holder.

RIGHT FRONT

Using the long-tail method, CO 44 (46, 50, 52, 54, 56, 58) sts. Beg and ending where indicated for your size (see Notes), work in patt from Basketweave chart until piece measures 5 (5, 5½, 5½, 6, 6, 6)" (12.5 [12.5, 14, 14, 15, 15, 15] cm), ending with a RS row.

Shape Armhole and Neck

BO 5 (5, 5, 6, 7, 8, 8) sts at beg of next WS row, work in patt to end—39 (41, 45, 46, 47, 48, 50) sts.

Note: Neck shaping is introduced while the armhole shaping is still in progress for some sizes; read the next sections all the way through before proceeding.

Dec row: (RS) Work in patt to last 2 sts, k2tog—1 st dec'd.

Basketweave Chart

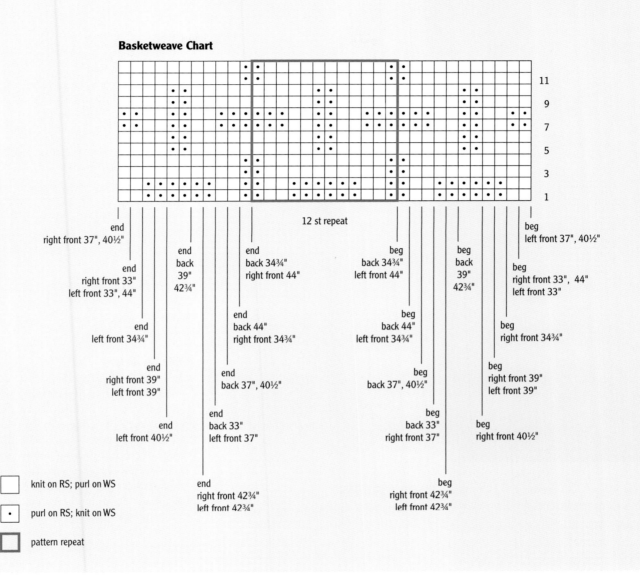

12 st repeat

end
right front 37", 40½"

end
right front 33"
left front 33", 44"

end
back
39"
42¾"

end
back 34¾"
right front 44"

beg
back 34¾"
left front 44"

beg
back
39"
42¾"

beg
left front 37", 40½"

beg
right front 33", 44"
left front 33"

end
left front 34¾"

end
back 44"
right front 34¾"

beg
back 44"
left front 34¾"

beg
right front 34¾"

end
right front 39"
left front 39"

end
back 37", 40½"

beg
back 37", 40½"

beg
right front 39"
left front 39"

end
left front 40½"

end
back 33"
left front 37"

beg
back 33"
right front 37"

beg
right front 40½"

knit on RS; purl on WS

· purl on RS; knit on WS

pattern repeat

end
right front 42¾"
left front 42¾"

beg
right front 42¾"
left front 42¾"

[Work 1 WS row even, then rep the dec row] 3 (3, 3, 4, 5, 6, 7) times, and at the same time, when armhole measures 1½" (3.8 cm) for all sizes BO 19 (21, 23, 23, 23, 23, 23) sts at beg of next RS row for neck shaping—16 (16, 18, 18, 18, 18, 19) sts rem after all armhole and neck shaping has been completed. Work even in patt until armhole measures 7½ (7½, 8, 8, 8½, 8½, 9)" (19 [19, 20.5, 20.5,

21.5, 21.5, 23] cm), ending with a WS row. Place all sts on scrap yarn holder.

LEFT FRONT
Using the long-tail method, CO 44 (46, 50, 52, 54, 56, 58) sts. Beg and ending where indicated for your size, work in patt from Basketweave chart until piece measures 5 (5, 5½, 5½, 6, 6, 6)" (12.5

[12.5, 14, 14, 15, 15, 15] cm), ending with a WS row.

Shape Armhole and Neck
BO 5 (5, 5, 6, 7, 8, 8) sts at beg of next RS row, work in patt to end—39 (41, 45, 46, 47, 48, 50) sts. Work 1 WS row even.

Note: As for the right front, the neck shaping is introduced while the armhole shaping is

Shape Sleeve Cap

BO 3 sts at beg of next 2 (2, 2, 2, 4, 4, 4) rows—62 (62, 64, 64, 62, 62, 64) sts. BO 2 sts at beg of next 4 (4, 4, 4, 2, 2, 2) rows—54 (54, 56, 56, 58, 58, 60) sts.

Dec row: (RS) K1, ssk, knit to last 3 sts, k2tog, k1—2 sts dec'd.

[Work 1 WS row even, then rep the dec row] 11 (11, 12, 12, 13, 13, 14) times—30 sts rem for all sizes. BO 2 sts at beg of next 4 rows—22 sts. BO 3 sts at beg of next 2 rows—16 sts. BO all sts.

FINISHING

Using wet-towel method, block all pieces to measurements. Let dry completely.

Join Shoulders

Place all back sts on main cir needle, then place right and left front shoulder sts on spare needle, making sure that the center front edges meet. Hold needles together and parallel with right sides of pieces touching and wrong sides facing out. Join yarn to armhole edge at start of right front shoulder sts. With one tip of main needle, use the three-needle bind-off method to join 16 (16, 18, 18, 18, 18, 19) back sts to right front shoulder sts. Using the same ball of yarn, BO the next 40 (46, 46, 48, 50, 52, 52) center back sts. With the same ball of yarn, use the three-needle bind-off to join rem back sts to 16 (16, 18, 18, 18, 18, 19) left front shoulder sts.

Sew side seams and sleeve seams using mattress st with ½-st seam allowances. Set sleeves into armholes, matching body side seams to sleeve seams, and center of each sleeve cap to shoulder seam. Pin in place with RS tog, easing fullness of sleeve cap to fit armhole. Working from WS, use slipstitch

still in progress for some sizes; read the next sections all the way through before proceeding.

Dec row: (RS) Ssk, work in patt to end—1 st dec'd.

[Work 1 WS row even, then rep the dec row] 3 (3, 3, 4, 5, 6, 7) times, and at the same time, when armhole measures 1½" (3.8 cm) for all sizes, BO 19 (21, 23, 23, 23, 23, 23) sts at beg of next WS row for neck shaping—16 (16, 18, 18, 18, 18, 19) sts rem after all armhole and neck shaping has been completed. Work even in patt until armhole measures 7½ (7½, 8, 8, 8½, 8½, 9)" (19 [19, 20.5, 20.5, 21.5, 21.5, 23] cm), ending with a WS row. Place all sts on scrap yarn holder.

SLEEVES

Using the long-tail method, CO 42 (42, 44, 44, 48, 48, 50) sts. Purl 1 RS row, knit 2 rows, purl 2 rows, then knit 1 WS row. Change to St st and work even for 8 rows, ending with a WS row—piece measures about 2" (5 cm) from CO.

Inc row: (RS) K1f&b, knit to last 2 sts, k1f&b, k1 (see Notes)—2 sts inc'd.

[Work even in St st for 7 rows, then rep the inc row] 12 times for all sizes—68 (68, 70, 70, 74, 74, 76) sts. Work even in St st until sleeve measures 17 (17, 17½, 17½, 17½, 17½, 18)" (43 [43, 44.5, 44.5, 44.5, 44.5, 45.5] cm) from CO, ending with a WS row.

crochet to seam sleeves to armholes, working with the body side of the seam facing you.

Front and Neck Band

With main cir needle and beg at lower right front corner, pick up and knit 33 (33, 36, 36, 39, 39, 39) sts along right center front edge to neck shaping, place marker (pm) for outer corner, 15 (17, 19, 19, 19, 19, 19) sts across right front neck BO edge to inner corner, pm, 31 (31, 33, 33, 36, 36, 38) along right front neck from inner corner to shoulder seam, 39 (45, 45, 47, 49, 51, 51) sts across back neck BO, 31 (31, 33, 33, 36, 36, 38) along left front neck edge from shoulder seam to inner corner, pm, 15 (17, 19, 19, 19, 19, 19) sts across left front neck BO edge from inner corner to left center front edge, pm, and 33 (33, 36, 36, 39, 39, 39) sts along left center front edge to end at lower left front corner—197 (207, 221, 223, 237, 239, 243) sts. Work as foll:

Row 1: (WS) Knit.

Row 2: (RS) Purl to first m, sl m, ★purl to 2 sts before next m (inner corner), p2tog, sl m, p2tog; rep from ★ once more, purl to end—4 sts dec'd, 1 st on each side of both inner corner m.

Row 3: Purl to first m (outer corner), ★M1P, sl m, M1P,★ purl across left neck, back neck, and right neck to second outer corner m, rep from ★ to ★, purl to end—4 sts inc'd, 1 st on each side of both outer corner m.

Row 4: (RS, buttonhole row) K2 (2, 2, 2, 4, 4, 4), yo, k2tog, [k5 (5, 6, 6, 6, 6, 6), yo, k2tog] 4 times, ★knit to 2 sts before inner corner m, ssk, sl m, k2tog; rep from ★ once more, knit to end—5 buttonholes completed; 4 sts dec'd, 1 st on each side of both inner corner m.

Row 5: Knit to first outer corner m, ★M1, sl m, M1,★ knit across left neck, back neck, and right neck to second outer corner m, rep from ★ to ★, knit

to end—4 sts inc'd, 1 st on each side of both outer corner m.

Row 6: Purl.

BO all sts kwise on next WS row.

Weave in ends. Lightly steam seams, being careful not to flatten the textured pattern. Sew buttons to left front, opposite buttonholes and centered in the St st "valley" of front band Rows 3 and 4. ❧

VICKI SQUARE combines her passion for knitting, her love of historic costume, and her vision for contemporary design into wearable knits for today. She is the author of several books, including the best-selling *Knitter's Companion Deluxe Edition with DVD* (Interweave, 2010), and her newest release *Light and Layered Knits* (Interweave, 2013).

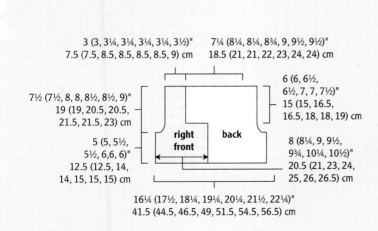

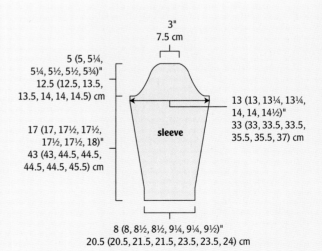

Sweetheart Bag

DONA KAY

Could a reticule serve more than one purpose? Perhaps Catherine Morland of *Northanger Abbey* carried such a bag—the heart-shaped vine intertwined with leaves and flowers carrying a subtle message of one looking for love. Who will notice? Certainly not someone as boorish as Mr. Thorpe, but perhaps the observant Mr. Tilney? The bag is worked circularly from lace top to shaped bottom with a simple I-cord drawstring. The motif is adapted for knitting from a sixteenth-century embroidery pattern.

FINISHED SIZE 14¾" (37.5 cm) circumference and 7¾" (19.5 cm) tall.

YARN Fingering weight (#1 Super Fine) *Shown here:* Jamieson's Shetland Spindrift (100% Shetland; 115 yd [105 m]/⅞ oz [25 g]): #815 ivy (A), #140 rye (B), 1 ball each. Distributed by Simply Shetland.

NEEDLES Size 2 (2.75 mm): 16" (40.5 cm) circular (cir) and double-pointed (dpn). Adjust needle size if necessary to obtain the correct gauge.

NOTIONS Markers (m); tapestry needle.

GAUGE 31 sts and 35 rnds = 4" (10 cm) measured over blocked bag chart.

Notes

◆ The color pattern has some areas with long stretches of one color. Weave in the stranded color in every five or six stitches in these areas.

◆ When the knitting is done use a damp cloth and an iron on wool setting to press the colorwork on both sides to "full" the knitting. Use the steam iron only (do not press) on the lace portion of the bag.

EDGING

With color B and cir needle, CO 120 sts. Pm and join in a rnd, being careful not to twist sts. Purl 1 rnd and break color B. Join color A and work 11 rnds of Lace Edging chart.

Eyelet rnd: ★K3, k2tog, [yo] twice, ssk, k3; rep from ★ around—12 eyelets.

Next rnd: ★K4, [k1, p1] into double yo, k4; rep from ★ around. Knit 1 rnd, purl 1 rnd. Change to dpns.

Dec rnd: ★K10, k2tog, [k17, k2tog] twice, k10, pm for side; rep from ★ once more—114 sts rem.

BODY

Join color B and work Rnds 1–53 of Bag chart, working the 57-st chart twice per rnd. When chart is complete

62 sts rem. Divide the sts of the front and back onto 2 dpn, hold work with RS tog and join using three-needle BO (see Glossary).

FINISHING

Weave in any loose ends. Block bag to measurements (see Notes). Using color B and dpn, knit a 36" (91.5 cm) 2-st I-cord (see Glossary) and BO. Weave cord through eyelets and sew CO and BO ends together. ✤

DONNA KAY of Barrington, New Hampshire, is an instructor, knitwear designer, and handspinner. Her passion for traditional knitting led her to start her own company, Tree of Life Designs. See more of her work at treeoflifedesigns.co.

Lace Edging Chart

	knit
•	purl
o	yo
⋏	sl1-k2tog-psso

✕	with color A, knit
	with color B, knit
╱	k2tog in indicated color
╲	ssk in indicated color
▦	no stitch

Bag Chart

53
51
49
47
45
43
41
39
37
35
33
31
29
27
25
23
21
19
17
15
13
11
9
7
5
3
1

Order Number: 82269475

Title: The Best Of Jane Austen Knits: 27 Regency-Inspired Designs

SKU: PB-LN-1620338815

Special: Amazon/112-7678079-0390656

Recipient: Jennifer Feit
3485 N SUNDOWN LN
OCEANSIDECA, US 92056-4710

Shipping Method: Standard

Buyer: Jennifer L Feit, dglz6swp397sx73@marketplace.

Quantity: 1

Location: [AA-9-16-1-1~]

Important Notice to All Customers

Bellwether Books has made every effort to inspect each book prior to shipment to ensure there are no markings and/or inscriptions of an offensive nature in the book you have purchased. However, the majorities of our titles are publisher returns, and while appearing in 'like new' condition, they may have some markings that we did not catch.

If you do find offensive markings in this book, please return the book and upon receipt back to us, we will ship another copy, if available, to you at no additional charge, or credit your account back the full amount (purchase price plus shipping & handling) should this copy be unavailable.

Thanks for purchasing from Bellwether Books, and we hope you enjoy your book!

For any questions or concerns, kindly email us at info@bellwetherbookstore.com

Margaret Dashwood Shawl

JOANNA JOHNSON

Joanna Johnson designed this sweet rustic lace shawl with young Margaret Dashwood of *Sense and Sensibility* in mind. One of the first things a young lady in reduced circumstances (living in a drafty cottage by the sea, no less) would need for her wardrobe is a pretty but functional everyday shawl. The shawl is worked from side to side, and the garter and lace edging is a perfect match for the airy woolen-spun yarn. Sized to fit a girl or young teen in a cross-back sontag style, this shawl also has enough length to be worn across the shoulders by knitters of any size.

FINISHED SIZE About 12" (30.5 cm) wide at center back and 74" (188 cm) long.

YARN Fingering weight (#1 Super Fine) *Shown here:* Brooklyn Tweed Loft (100% Targhee-Columbia wool; 275 yd [251 m]/1¾ oz [50 g]): #07 thistle, 2 skeins.

NEEDLES Size 6 (4 mm): straight or circular (cir). Adjust needle size if necessary to obtain the correct gauge.

NOTIONS Marker (m).

GAUGE 22 sts and 34 rows = 4" (10 cm) in Garter st.

Notes

◆ This rustic lace and garter shawl is worked from side to side, beginning at one edge, increasing in width as you approach the center of the back. It is then gradually decreased and cast off at the other side. Using very basic lace and shaping techniques worked over a 10-row repeat, it is an ideal first shawl for a beginning knitter.

◆ Slip stitches purlwise with yarn in back.

SHAWL

CO 26 sts.

Set-up row: (WS) K19, pm, p1, k6.

10-Row Increase

Begin working the 10-row increasing patt as foll:

Note: St count changes each row but only 1 st is dec'd over the entire 10-row patt.

Row 1: (RS) Knit to 1 st before m, sl 1, sl m, k3, [yo, k2tog] 7 times, yo, k2—1st inc'd.

Rows 2, 4, 6, and 8: Knit to m, sl m, p1, knit to end of row.

Row 3: Knit to 1 st before m, sl 1, sl m, k6, [yo, k2tog] 6 times, yo, k2—1 st inc'd.

Row 5: Knit to 1 st before m, sl 1, sl m, k9 [yo, k2tog] 5 times, yo, k2—1 st inc'd.

Row 7: Knit to 1 st before m, sl 1, sl m, k12 [yo, k2tog] 4 times, yo, k2—1 st inc'd.

Row 9: Knit to 2 sts before marker, k1f&b, sl 1, sl m, k23—1 st inc'd.

Row 10: BO 4 sts, knit to m, sl m, p1, knit to end of row—4 sts dec'd; 1 st inc'd over 10-row patt.

Repeat Rows 1–10 thirty more times—57 sts.

10-Row Decrease

Begin working 10-row decreasing patt as foll:

Note: St count changes each row but only 1 st is dec'd over the entire 10-row patt.

Row 1: (RS) Knit to 1 st before m, sl 1, sl m, k3, [yo, k2tog] 7 times, yo, k2—1 st inc'd.

Rows 2, 4, 6, and 8: Knit to marker, sl m, p1, knit to end of row.

Row 3: Knit to 1 st before m, sl 1, sl m, k6, [yo, k2tog] 6 times, yo, k2—1 st inc'd.

Row 5: Knit to 1 st before m, sl 1, sl m, k9 [yo, k2tog] 5 times, yo, k2—1 st inc'd.

Row 7: Knit to 1 st before m, sl 1, sl m, k12 [yo, k2tog] 4 times, yo, k2—1 st inc'd.

Row 9: Knit to 3 sts before m, k2tog, sl 1, sl m, k23—1 st dec'd.

Row 10: BO 4 sts, knit to m, sl m, p1, knit to end of row—4 sts dec'd; 1 st dec'd over 10-row patt.

Repeat Rows 1–10 thirty more times—26 sts.

BO all sts loosely.

FINISHING

Weave in ends. Block to measurements. ❦

JOANNA JOHNSON is the author and pattern designer of the knitting picture books *Phoebe's Sweater, Freddie's Blanket,* and *Phoebe's Birthday,* which are illustrated by her husband, Eric, and published by their independent press, Slate Falls Press (slatefallspress.com). She enjoys working with what she believes to be the perfect combination of materials: books and yarn.

WHERE *Jane* LIVED

BY SHERYL CRAIG

Elinor and Marianne Dashwood in *Sense and Sensibility,* Fanny Price in *Mansfield Park,* Jane Fairfax in *Emma,* and Anne Elliot in *Persuasion* all lose their family homes, a deprivation that Jane Austen experienced herself. After spending the first twenty-five years of her life living in the house where she was born, Jane would change homes six times in the next nine years. Jane's last move, into a sturdy brick house on the edge of the village of Chawton in 1809, came as a great relief and a return to stability.

Jane Austen was born in 1775 in the church rectory near the village of Steventon in Hampshire, England, where her father was the local Church of England clergyman and a relative of the principal landowner in the parish. On Sundays, the Reverend George Austen delivered his weekly sermons, but he was also Farmer Austen during the week. The Austens had a large garden on three acres of land that surrounded the rectory, but Mr. Austen also rented two hundred acres of farmland nearby where he grew wheat, barley, oats, hops, and fruit trees and kept cows, sheep, poultry, and bees. The parsonage house was demolished in 1824, a few years after Jane's death, and today the empty field is a cow pasture.

The field in Steventon, the site of the house where Jane Austen was born and lived for the first twenty-five years of her life.

Jane Austen's house in Chawton, England (shown above and opposite). When the windows are open in the house, you can hear the sheep in the field just down the road.

The few drawings of the Steventon rectory that have survived vary, so we don't know for certain how large the house really was. As the Austens had eight children, presumably, the bigger, the better. We now know more however, as a team of archaeologists excavated the field in 2011 and began exhibiting their finds in 2012. We do know that the house was old-fashioned, with exposed beams and casement windows, and the front door opened directly into a sitting room, just like in a laborer's cottage, so someone like *Pride and Prejudice*'s Lady Catherine would not have been impressed, had she condescended to pay a call. The cellar had a tendency to flood, but none of the rectory's inconveniences mattered much to Jane who was very fond of her childhood home.

In 1800, Jane's father probably suffered either a heart attack or a stroke and decided to retire and move with his wife and daughters to Bath. Jane had vacationed in Bath with her uncle and aunt, and, like Catherine Morland in *Northanger Abbey,* enjoyed her visits, but Jane had no desire to permanently live there. When Jane was told that her parents planned to leave Steventon, family legend has it that she fainted. The house Mr. Austen leased at 4 Sydney Place in 1801 was on the outskirts of Bath, and the tall windows of the drawing room looked out on the newly planted Sydney Gardens. Bath was, and still is, a tourist mecca with concerts, balls, plays, lectures, recitals, and enticing shops. But all of that entertainment cost money, and the Austens' disposable income was in short supply.

Unfortunately, the Sydney Place house was more expensive than the Austens could afford, so, as soon as their lease was up, they moved into a cheaper house. When George Austen died in 1805, most of the family's income went with him, and his widow and daughters were forced to further economize. They moved twice in the next eighteen months and were finally renting only a few rooms. Money, or more precisely, the lack of it, had become a major preoccupation.

In 1806, the three Austen ladies and Martha Lloyd, an old family friend, moved in with one of Jane's brothers, naval Captain Francis Austen, and his wife, Mary, who were living in the port town of Southampton. Frank and his mother pooled their resources to rent a pleasant house with a garden. The Austens seemed happy during their three years in Southampton, and Jane's socializing with sailors and

The Chawton Great House, now the Chawton House Library, the smaller of Edward Austen's two manor houses.

Some of the Austens' furniture remains, including the table on which Jane wrote, and Jane's bed has been replicated. Period antiques fill in empty spaces to suggest how the areas may have been furnished. A lock of Jane's hair is on display as well as other personal items. There are also samples of Jane's sewing and embroidery and a patchwork quilt stitched by Jane, her mother, and sister.

A visit to Chawton Cottage is altogether a treat. Not only is there so much to see, but fragrant, fresh-cut flowers from the garden fill vases in the rooms, and some of the same sounds that Jane Austen heard still echo through the peaceful house.

their families would be useful when she wrote *Persuasion*. When Frank and Mary moved to the Isle of Wight, Jane was uprooted once again. But this time, Mrs. Austen was offered a house, rent free.

Edward Austen, another of Jane's brothers, had been legally adopted by wealthy, childless relatives, the Knights, and Edward Austen Knight inherited two estates when his adoptive father died. Edward offered his mother her choice of two houses, one on his larger estate in Kent and the other on his smaller estate in Hampshire. Mrs. Austen chose Chawton Cottage, no doubt because in Hampshire they were closer to Jane's eldest brother, James, and to their old friends at Steventon.

Chawton Cottage had originally been a coaching inn, but as a house, it was ideal for the Austen ladies. Edward Austen Knight's manor house and the village church are only a pleasant stroll away. When Jane wrote a letter to Frank, she added a poetic tribute: "Our Chawton home, how

much we find/Already in it to our mind/And how convinced, that when complete/It will all other houses beat." On a small table next to the dining room window, Jane took advantage of the privacy and light to write and revise her novels. To add to Jane's happiness, eventually Frank and Mary rented a house in the nearby town of Alton, and Jane's brother Henry was appointed curate at Chawton parish. Chawton Cottage remained Jane's home until she died in 1817.

Today, Chawton Cottage is known as Jane Austen's House Museum and is open to the public. The village of Chawton looks much as it did in the early nineteenth century when about four hundred people lived there, and the fortunate visitor to Jane Austen's house has the distinct feeling of leaving the twenty-first century behind. The former stable that housed the Austens' donkeys is now a gift shop, and a visitors' center has been built in the garden, but the house has been lovingly restored and is very much as it was when Jane lived there.

The Jane Austen Centre on Gay Street in Bath. Jane Austen lived on Gay Street at one point, just a couple of doors down from the Jane Austen Centre.

When the windows are open in fine weather, visitors can hear the bleating of sheep in a nearby field, and in the afternoons, the clip-clop of the Chawton Pony Club riding past the house reminds us of the pace of life when Jane Austen was alive. Visitors who are musical are encouraged to play some of Jane's favorite songs on the 1810 Clementi piano. On inclement days, it is not at all difficult to imagine Jane Austen sitting near the fireplace in the parlor and knitting, with ink-stained fingers, of course.

For a virtual tour of Jane Austen's home at Chawton Cottage, go to jane-austens-house-museum.org.uk.

SHERYL CRAIG has a PhD in nineteenth-century British literature from the University of Kansas, and she teaches English at the University of Central Missouri. She has published dozens of articles in *Jane Austen's Regency World* magazine. Sheryl is a life member of the Jane Austen Society of North America (JASNA) and the editor of the society's newsletter, JASNA News.

The church at Chawton where Jane's brother Henry was the curate; it is just down the road from the Jane Austen's House Museum.

Shape Cap

Shape cap with short rows as foll:

Short-row 1: With RS facing, knit to 2nd mC, knitting all yos of previous row tbl, sl m, w&t so WS is facing, purl to 1st mC, sl m, w&t.

Short-row 2: With RS facing, knit to wrapped st of row below, knit wrapped st working it tog with the wrap, w&t so WS is facing, purl to wrapped st of row below, purl wrapped st working it tog with the wrap, w&t. Rep Short-row 2 until you reach mB on both sides of armhole.

Next rnd: With RS facing, knit to end of rnd. Knit 5 (5, 6, 6, 7) rnds.

Dec rnd 1: Knit to first mC, sl m, k0 (1, 0, 2, 0), [k2tog, k1] 10 (10, 12, 11, 14) times, k2tog, knit to end—79 (85, 93, 100, 109) sts rem.

Dec rnd 2: (Remove all m as you come to them), knit to first mB, k7 (8, 6, 11, 8), [k2tog, k1] 4 (4, 5, 4, 4) times, [sl 1, k2tog, psso] 7 times, [k1, k2tog] 4 (4, 5, 4, 4) times, knit to end—57 (63, 69, 78, 87) sts rem.

Edging

With CC and smaller dpn, purl.

Next rnd: (WS) [K3tog tbl leaving sts on left needle, yo] 2 times, k3tog tbl then sl sts of left needle, ★yo, [k3tog tbl leaving sts on left needle, yo] 2 times, k3tog tbl then sl sts of left needle; rep from ★ to end. BO all sts kwise.

FINISHING

Carefully remove waste yarn from Provisional CO sts at CO edge of Lower Body, fold back CO edge at turning row and invisibly whipstitch live sts to WS.

Upper Body Edging

With CC, smaller cir, and RS facing, beg at right belt, pick up and k87 (91, 95, 100, 108) sts evenly along right front to shoulder, 39 (43, 47, 49, 51) sts along back neck, and 87 (91, 95, 100, 108) sts down left front to left belt—213 (225, 237, 249, 267) sts.

Row 1: (WS) [K3tog tbl leaving sts on left needle, yo] 2 times, k3tog tbl, then sl sts of left needle, ★yo, [k3tog tbl leaving sts on left needle, yo] 2 times, k3tog tbl, then sl sts of left needle; rep from ★ to end—355 (375, 395, 415, 445) sts. BO all sts kwise.

Lower Right Front Edging

With CC, smaller cir and RS facing, beg at lower edge of Lower Right Front pick up and knit 36 sts to right belt. Cont as for upper body edging.

Lower Left Front Edging

With CC, smaller cir and RS facing, beg at belt of Lower Left Front pick up and knit 36 sts to lower edge. Cont as for upper body edging. Weave in ends. Block lightly to measurements. ✦

CLAUDIA GEIGER knits and spins in Berne, Switzerland. One of her favorite Jane Austen moments is from the 1995 BBC production of *Pride and Prejudice,* when Lizzy Bennet exclaims, "Shelves in the closet—happy thought indeed!"

Bonnet & Wristlets for Baby Emma

SUSAN STRAWN

Emma Woodhouse of Jane Austen's *Emma* was born to a life of wealth and privilege, a fortunate child indulged by an affectionate father. Emma's mother may have knitted such finery as this baby bonnet and wristlets for her precious infant. When Emma grew to young womanhood, she had no need or desire to marry, and she did not anticipate babes of her own. Instead, she saved the delicate bonnet for her niece and namesake, baby Emma.

FINISHED SIZES
Newborn (6 months–1 year).
Bonnet: About 5 (6¼)" (12.5 [16] cm) wide and 5½ (6¾)" (14 [17] cm) tall.
Wristlet: About 3¼ (4¼)" (8.5 [11] cm) circumference.

YARN Fingering weight (#1 Super Fine) *Shown here:* Schoeller Stahl Fortissima Socka 100 (75% superwash wool, 25% polyamide; 458 yd [420 m]/3½ oz [100 g]): #2001 white, 1 skein. Distributed by Skacel.

NEEDLES Size 1 (2.25 mm) set of 5 double-pointed (dpn). Adjust needle sizes if necessary to obtain the correct gauge.

NOTIONS Stitch markers (m); tapestry needle; ⅜" (1 cm) satin ribbon, 1 yd (1 m).

GAUGE 34 sts and 56 rows = 4" (10 cm) in Openwork Diamonds patt.

BONNET BACK

CO 8 sts and divide sts equally onto 4 dpn. Pm and join to work in the rnd being careful not to twist sts. Work Rnds 1–23 (1–27) of Back chart for your size—96 (112) sts, end the last rnd 3 (1) st(s) before m. BO 17 (15) sts removing m—79 (97) sts.

LACE PORTION

Change to 3 dpn and knit back and forth instead of around. Work Rows 1–8 of Openwork Diamonds chart 4 (6) times. Knit 3 rows.

BORDER

Change to 5 dpn, pm for corner, with RS facing, pick up and knit 16 (23)

sts evenly along selvedge edge of lace, 17 (15) sts along back BO sts, then 17 (23) sts along other selvedge edge of lace—129 (158) sts. Pm for beg of rnd and join to work in the rnd. Purl 1 rnd. Knit 1 rnd.

Inc rnd: Knit to m, remove m, M1, knit to end of rnd, M1—131 (160) sts.

Eyelet rnd: *K3, yo, k2tog, rep from * to last 1 (0) sts, k1 (0)—26 (32) eyelets.

Knit 3 rnds, *purl 1 rnd, knit 1 rnd, rep from * 1 more time.

Picot BO

Picot BO as follows:

*Use knitted method (see Glossary) to CO 2 sts, BO 5 sts, then sl the st on the right needle onto the left needle; rep from * 26 (32) more times—50 (61) sts rem. BO rem sts.

BONNET FINISHING

Block piece to measurements. Weave in loose ends. Thread satin ribbon through eyelets along neck (edge without picots).

WRISTLET (make 2)

CO 27 (36) sts and divide sts equally onto 3 dpn. Pm and join to work in the rnd being careful not to twist sts.

*Purl 1 rnd, knit 1 rnd; rep from * 2 more times. Work in St st until piece measures 1½" (3.8 cm) from beg. *Purl 1 rnd, knit 1 rnd; rep from * 1 more time. Knit 1 rnd.

Eyelet rnd: *K1, yo, k2tog; rep from *—9 (12) eyelets.

Knit 3 rnds.

*Purl 1 rnd, knit 1 rnd; rep from * 1 more time.

Picot BO

Picot BO as follows:

⋆Use the knitted method to CO 2 sts, BO 5 sts, then sl the st on the right needle onto the left needle; rep from ⋆ 8 (11) more times.

WRISTLET FINISHING

Block piece to measurements. Weave in loose ends. ⋆

SUSAN STRAWN lives in Oak Park, Illinois, where she is a professor at Dominican University in River Forest. During summers, she knits in Seattle. She is the author of *Knitting America, A Glorious History from Warm Socks to High Art* (Voyageur Press, 2007).

Newborn Back Chart

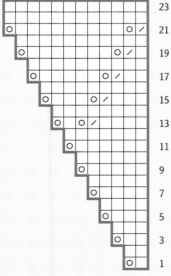

23
21
19
17
15
13
11
9
7
5
3
1

6 months–1 year Back Chart

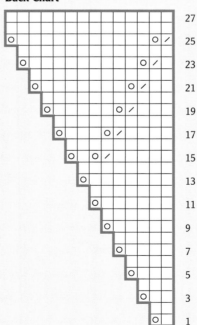

27
25
23
21
19
17
15
13
11
9
7
5
3
1

Openwork Diamonds Chart

7
5
3
1

☐ knit

⊙ yo

╱ k2tog

╲ ssk

⋀ sl2tog-k1-p2sso

☐ pattern repeat

[k2, p2] 13 times, k2, p1—112 sts rem.

SIZE 34½ ONLY
P2tog, k2tog, k1, [p2, k2] 5 times, [p2tog] 2 times, k2, p2, [k2, p1, p2tog] 6 times, k2, p2, k2, [p2tog] 2 times, [k2, p2] 5 times, k2, [p2tog] 2 times, [k2, p2] 8 times, k2, p1—120 sts rem.

SIZE 38¼ ONLY
P2tog, [k2, p2] 6 times, [k2, p1, p2tog] 9 times, k2, p2, k2, p1, p2tog, [k2, p2] 6 times, k2, p1, p2tog, [k2, p2] 9 times, k2, p1—136 sts rem.

SIZE 43¼ ONLY
[P2, k2] 9 times, [p1, p2tog, k2] 11 times, [p2, k2] 20 times—160 sts rem.

ALL SIZES
Work 4 rnds in established patt. BO all sts in patt.

FINISHING

For each underarm, return 12 (14, 16, 18, 20) held sts from body onto dpn, and 12 (14, 16, 18, 20) held sts from sleeve onto second dpn. Graft together using the Kitchener stitch (see Glossary). Weave in all ends. Block to measurements. ❧

KATHLEEN DAMES designs and knits in New York City and Bath, Maine, with her very own Captain Wentworth and their three children. All of Jane Austen's works have provided her with joy and inspiration. You can find more of Kathleen's designs at kathleendames.blogspot.com, and she goes by the username Purly on Ravelry.

orate
d Craf

A Book Cover for Edmund

MELISSA J. ARMSTRONG

It is easy to imagine Fanny Price of *Mansfield Park* knitting Edmund a Bible cover as a gift for his ordination, a gift of support as he struggled with his vows and conflict over feelings for Miss Crawford. As a further reminder of their enduring friendship, the book cover features a ribbed horseshoe cable, reflecting the gratitude Fanny had for Edmund's help in overcoming her fear of horses. This resizable book cover can serve the modern knitter as a cover for an Austen novel or a well-loved journal, a possession treasured by many an Austen heroine.

FINISHED SIZES 12½" (31.5 cm) wide, 7½" (19 cm) tall. Instructions are provided to adjust the size to cover your specific book.

YARN Worsted weight (#4 Medium) *Shown here:* Brown Sheep Company Lamb's Pride (85% wool, 15% mohair; 190 yd [173 m]/113 g): spice, 1 skein for given size (more may be needed for a larger book).

NEEDLES Size 3 (3.25 mm). Adjust needle size if necessary to obtain the correct gauge.

NOTIONS Cable needle (cn); stitch markers (m); tapestry needle.

GAUGE 18 sts and 29 rows = 4" (10 cm) in rev St st; 16 sts in Ribbed Horseshoe chart = 1¾" (4.5 cm).

Notes

◆ *Directions are given for one size, with instructions on how to modify the pattern for other book sizes. While there is a little bit of stretch in the book cover with the recommended yarn, the cover fits awkwardly if forced to stretch too much. Knit your book cover to your measured size, erring on the side of the cover being slightly larger than the book.*

◆ *It is particularly important to wash and block your swatch, because in a small item such as this, correct gauge is critical to success.*

◆ *Make a swatch in both rev St st and Ribbed Horseshoe to double check your calculation for the number of sts and rows needed.*

Customize for Your Book

Measure the size of the book that you want to cover and note dimensions:

_____ Width (binding to opening)

_____ Depth (binding width)

_____ Height (bottom to top)

For provided size, 5½" (14 cm) wide; 1½" (3.8 cm) high; 7½" (19 cm) long.

TO DETERMINE THE TOTAL NUMBER OF CO STS:

_____ = Front cover CO: To determine the approximate number of sts that cover the front of the book, multiply the book width by the st gauge per 1" (2.5 cm) add 9 sts to compensate for the horseshoe ribbing (e.g., 5½" [14 cm] × 4½ = 24¾; + 9 = 33¾ sts; rounded to the nearest whole number = 34 sts).

_____ = Binding CO: To determine the number of sts that cover the binding, multiply the binding depth by the st gauge per 1" (2.5 cm) (e.g., 1½" [3.8 cm] × 4½ = 6¾ sts; rounded to the nearest whole number = 7 sts).

_____ = Back cover CO: To determine the approximate number of sts that cover the back of the book, multiply the book width by the st gauge per 1" (2.5 cm) (e.g., 5½" [14 cm] × 4½ = 24¾; rounded to the nearest whole number = 25 sts).

_____ = Total CO: Add the Front cover CO, the Binding CO and the Back cover CO together (e.g., 34 + 7 + 25 = 66 sts).

TO DETERMINE THE PLACEMENT OF THE RIBBED HORSESHOE CHART:

_____ = Sts worked before Ribbed Horseshoe chart: To determine how many sts to work before the Ribbed Horseshoe

chart, subtract 16 chart sts from the front cover CO, then divide that sum by 2 (e.g., 34 front cover sts – 16 chart sts = 18 sts; ÷ 2 = 9 sts; if you get a half number, round down to the nearest whole number).

TO DETERMINE THE NUMBER OF 10-ROW CHART REPEATS AND WHETHER AN EDGING IS REQUIRED:

_____ = 10-Row repeats of Ribbed Horseshoe chart: To determine how many 10-Row repeats of the chart to work, multiply the length of the book by the rev St st row gauge per 1" (2.5 cm), then divide by 10 (e.g., 7½" [19 cm] × 7¼ = 54⅜; rounded to the nearest even whole number = 54 sts; ÷ 10 = 5 repeats, with a remainder of 4 sts).

_____ = Garter Ridges on each edge of chart: To determine how many garter ridges to work before and after the Ribbed Horseshoe chart, divide the remainder from the previous step by 2 (e.g., 4 sts ÷ 2 = 2 garter ridges before and after Ribbed Horseshoe chart). Note that each garter ridge is 2 rows.

TO DETERMINE THE PLACEMENT OF THE KEY HOLE:

_____ = Repeats worked before the keyhole: To determine how many repeats to work before the 10 keyhole rows, subtract 1 from the total number of repeats, then divide by 2 (e.g., 5 repeats – 1 = 4; ÷ 2 = 2 repeats; or 6 repeats – 1 = 5; ÷ 2 = 2½ repeats). For a whole repeat, begin the keyhole with Row 1 and end it with Row 10 of the same repeat. For half a repeat, begin the keyhole with Row 5 and end it with Row 4 of the following repeat.

COVER

CO the total number of sts _____ (e.g., 66 sts).

Work Garter Ridges: Knit _____ rows (e.g., 4), ending with a WS row.

Set Up Ribbed Horseshoe Chart

(RS) Work in rev St st (purl on RS, knit on WS) for _____ sts worked before Ribbed Horseshoe chart (e.g., 9), pm, work 16 sts in Ribbed Horseshoe chart, pm, work in rev St st to end. Cont in established patt for _____ repeats to the beg of the keyhole (e.g., 2), ending after WS Row 10 or 4 of chart.

Work Keyhole

For the first section, with RS facing work in rev St st to the first m, turn. Cont working just these sts for 8 more rows, ending with a RS row. Cut yarn, keep sts on needle.

For the second section, reattach the yarn and work the next row as charted to the next m, turn. Cont working just these 16 sts for 8 more rows, ending with a RS row. Cut yarn, keep sts on needle.

For the third section, reattach yarn and work in rev St st to end of row, turn. Cont working just these sts for 8 more rows, ending with a RS row.

Keyhole joining row: (WS) Work across all sts in pattern, reconnecting the 3 sections. Cont in patt until all _____ repeats of the Ribbed Horseshoe chart are completed (e.g., 5), ending with Row 10 of chart.

Work Garter Ridges

Knit _____ rows (e.g., 4), ending with a WS row. BO all sts knitwise.

CORNERS

Fold cover lengthwise into 3 equal sections. Place a removable m at each fold (2 on each edge) to mark placement of corners.

Back Lower Corner

Row 1: (RS) With RS facing and the back edge at the top, beg at left m, pick up and knit 1 sts for each row to the corner. Note number of sts: ____.

Row 2: (WS) Purl.

Row 3 (dec row): (RS) Ssk, knit to end—1 st dec'd.

Rep Rows 2 and 3 until 3 sts rem, ending with a WS row.

Next row: (RS) Sl 1, ssk, psso—1 st rem. Cut yarn and draw through last st, leaving about 12" (30.5 cm) tail for seaming.

Back Upper Corner

Row 1: (RS) With RS facing you and the back edge at the top, beg at the right corner, pick up and knit the same number of sts as for the back lower corner (about 1 st per row) until you reach the stitch marker.

Row 2: (WS) Purl.

Row 3: (RS) Knit to the last 2 sts, k2tog—1 st dec'd.

Rep Rows 2 and 3 until 3 st rem, ending with a WS row.

Next row: (RS) K3tog—1 st rem. Cut yarn and draw through last st, leaving about 12" (30.5 cm) tail for seaming.

Rotate book cover so that RS faces you and the front edge is at the top.

Front Lower Corner

Work as for back upper corner.

Front Upper Corner

Work as for back lower corner.

Use tails to sew side edges of each corner along the top and bottom edges of the cover.

With RS facing and the back edge at the top, determine the center of the back (this should line up with the keyhole on the front), pick up and knit 6 sts in the center of the back edge. Work in Garter st (knit every row) until piece is long enough to comfortably go through the keyhole on the front of the book cover (e.g., 4¾" [12 cm]), ending with a WS row:

Cast-on row 1: Knit to end, using the Backward-loop method (see Glossary), CO 3 sts—9 sts.

Rep Cast-on Row once more—12 sts. Knit 2 rows, ending with a WS row.

Dec row: (RS) K1, ssk, knit to last 3 sts, k2tog, k1—2 sts dec'd. Knit 1 WS row. Rep the last 2 rows 3 more times—4 sts rem.

Next row: (RS) K1, ssk, k1—3 sts rem. Knit 1 WS row.

Next row: (RS) Sl 1, k2tog, psso—1 st rem. Cut yarn and draw it through the last st.

FINISHING

Block to book measurements or slightly larger. Weave in loose ends.

If you choose to use a different weight yarn with a different gauge, you can do the calculations for your yarn gauge. Simply follow the instructions provided but substitute your gauge (e.g., 7 st/1" [2.5 cm]) for the gauge provided. Keep in mind that the pattern will work best at a tight gauge for good coverage of the book in a yarn with good stitch definition, a little stretch, and the ability to block well so that you can achieve the right fit for your book. ♣

MELISSA ARMSTRONG is a physician recently relocated to Baltimore, Maryland. Knitting and Jane Austen serve as two of her favorite ways to relax (often together). She thinks *Mansfield Park* is a sadly neglected book in many Austen libraries. She can be found as neurochick on Ravelry.

Ribbed Horseshoe Chart

	knit on RS, purl on WS
	purl on RS, knit on WS
	sl 4 sts onto cn and hold in back, k1, p2, k1 from left needle, k1, p2, k1 from cn
	sl 4 sts onto cn and hold in front, k1, p2, k1 from left needle, k1, p2, k1 from cn

Emma's Overdress

HEATHER ZOPPETTI

The overdress was the perfect cover-up to change the look of a simple day dress and to protect clothing from wear. Inspired by an overdress worn in the 1996 film adaptation of *Emma,* this design has been shortened into a tunic-length garment for modern women. Wear it over a shirt or sundress for added warmth and style. The cabled band is knitted first, and stitches are picked up for both the bodice and skirt. A dainty lace edging keeps the appearance feminine, and a pretty button closure adorns the front.

FINISHED SIZES 28 (32, 36, 39¾, 43¾, 47¾, 51¾)" (71 [81.5, 91.5, 101, 111] cm) bust circumference, buttoned. Vest shown measures 32" (81.5 cm).

YARN Sportweight (#2 Fine)
Shown here: Swans Island Natural Colors Collection (100% organic Merino; 525 yd [480 m]/3½ oz [100 g]): #YF120 winterberry, 2 (2, 2, 3, 3, 3, 3) skeins.

NEEDLES Cabled band—size 2 (2.75 mm); Body—size 4 (3.5 mm): 32" (81.5 cm) circular (cir). Adjust needle sizes if necessary to obtain the correct gauge.

NOTIONS Cable needle (cn); markers (m); stitch holders; tapestry needle; one ⅞" (2.2 cm) button.

GAUGE 28 sts and 38 rows = 4" (10 cm) in St st on larger needles.

Note

❖ *Because the border sts will vary in number depending on where you are in the chart, most st counts will be given discounting the borders.*

Stitch Guide

RIBBING

Row 1: Sl 1 pwise with yarn in front, * k1, p1; rep from * to last st, k1.

Rep Row 1 for patt.

WAISTBAND

With smaller needles, CO 20 sts. Work Ribbing (see Stitch Guide) until piece measures 1" (2.5 cm). Work Rows 1–8 of Cable chart 40 (47, 54, 60, 67, 74, 81) times. Work in Ribbing for ½" (1.3 cm) ending with a WS row.

Next row: (RS) Work 8 sts in patt, BO 4 sts, work in patt to end.

Next row: (WS) Work 8 sts in patt, CO 4 sts, work in patt to end. Work in patt until ribbing measures 1" (2.5 cm). BO all sts in patt. Waistband measures about 25 (29, 33, 36¼, 40¼, 44¼, 48¼)" (63.5 [73.5, 84, 92, 102, 112.5, 112.5, 122.5] cm).

SKIRT

With larger needles and RS of waistband facing, beg at CO end working bet ribbing on cable section only, pick up and knit 4 sts for left front border, pm, 34 (41, 48, 54, 61, 68, 75) sts for left front, pm for left side seam, 84 (98, 112, 124, 138, 152, 166) sts for back, pm for right side seam, 34 (41, 48, 54, 61, 68, 75) sts for right front, pm, 4 sts for right front border—160 (188, 216, 240, 268, 296, 324) sts.

Next row: (WS) Work Row 1 of Border A chart, sl m, purl to last m, sl m, work Row 1 of Border B chart.

Next row: (RS) Work next row of Border B chart, sl m, knit to last m, sl m, work next row of Border A chart.

Cont in patt as established, working in St st between border m, until piece measures 2" (5 cm) from pick up row, ending with a WS row.

Inc row: (RS) Work in patt to left side seam m, M1R (see Glossary), sl m, k1, M1L (see Glossary), work in patt to 1

st before right side seam m, M1R, k1, sl m, M1L, work in patt to end— 4 sts inc'd.

Cont in patt, rep Inc Row every 10th row 5 more times—176 (204, 232, 256, 284, 312, 340) sts between border m; 96 (110, 124, 136, 150, 164, 178) back sts and 40 (47, 54, 60, 67, 74, 81) sts each front. Work 1 WS row in patt.

Dec row: (RS) Work border sts in patt, sl m, k1, ssk, work in patt to 3 sts before border st m, k2tog, k1, sl m, work border sts in patt—2 sts dec'd.

Cont in patt, rep Dec row every 4th row 3 more times, then every RS row 10 times—148 (176, 204, 228, 256, 284, 312) sts rem between border m; 26 (33, 40, 46, 53, 60, 67) sts rem each front.

Next row: (WS) Work right front border sts in patt, BO 148 (176, 204, 228, 256, 284, 312) sts, work left front border sts in patt—only border sts rem. Place right front border sts on st holder.

Edging

Working on left front border sts, beg with next row in patt, rep Rows 6–9 of chart 52 (61, 71, 80, 90, 99, 109) more times, ending after last RS row where chart will best match rem sts from right front border—st counts for both borders should match.

Next row: (WS) K1, purl to end. Use Kitchener st (see Glossary) to graft left front border to right front border.

BODICE

With larger needles and RS of waistband facing, working bet ribbing on cable section only, pick up and knit 4 sts for right front border, pm, 34 (41, 48, 54, 61, 68, 75) sts for right front, pm for right side seam, 84 (98, 112,

124, 138, 152, 166) sts for back, pm for left side seam, 34 (41, 48, 54, 61, 68, 75) sts for left front, pm, 4 sts for left front border—160 (188, 216, 240, 268, 296, 324) sts.

Next row: (WS) Work Row 1 of Border A chart, sl m, purl to last m, sl m, work Row 1 of Border B chart.

Inc row: (RS) Work next row of Border B chart, sl m, knit to right side seam m, M1R, sl m, k1, M1L, work in patt to 1 st before left side seam m, M1R, k1, sl m, M1L, knit to last m, sl m, work next row of Border A chart—4 sts inc'd.

Cont in patt, rep Inc Row every 4th row 6 more times—180 (208, 236, 260, 288, 316, 344) sts between border m; 98 (112, 126, 138, 152, 166, 180) back sts and 41 (48, 55, 61, 68, 75, 82) sts each front. Work even in patt until bodice measures 3½" (9 cm) from pick-up row.

Separate Fronts and Back

(RS) Work border sts in patt, sl m, [knit to 7 (7, 7, 8, 8, 10, 10) sts before next m, BO 14 (14, 14, 16, 16, 20, 20) sts] twice, work in patt to end—84 (98, 112, 122, 136, 146, 160) back sts and 34 (41, 48, 53, 60, 65, 72) sts each front minus border sts. Place right front, including border, and back sts, including any m, on st holders.

LEFT FRONT

Next row: (WS) Work border sts in patt, sl m, work to end of row, pm, CO 4 sts for sleeve border.

Note: Armhole shaping and neckline shaping are worked simultaneously. Read through foll section before proceeding.

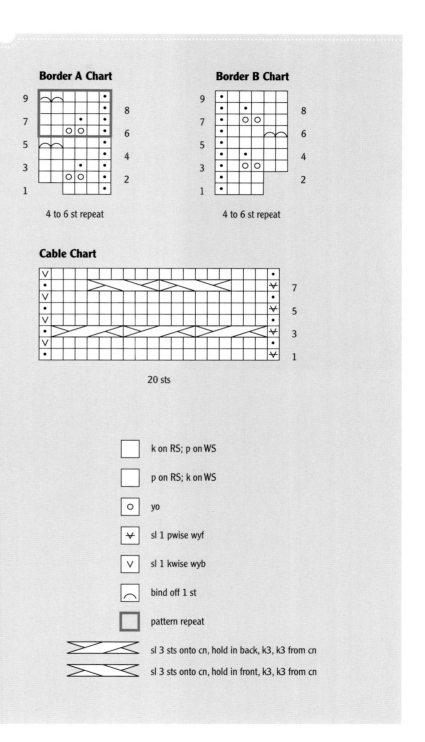

Border A Chart

4 to 6 st repeat

Border B Chart

4 to 6 st repeat

Cable Chart

20 sts

	k on RS; p on WS
	p on RS; k on WS
o	yo
⅄	sl 1 pwise wyf
v	sl 1 kwise wyb
⌒	bind off 1 st
	pattern repeat
	sl 3 sts onto cn, hold in back, k3, k3 from cn
	sl 3 sts onto cn, hold in front, k3, k3 from cn

Shape Armhole at the Beginning of the Row

(RS) Beg with Row 2, work next row of Border B chart, sl m, k1, ssk, work in patt to end of row—1 st dec'd. Work armhole dec every other row 9 (9, 11, 11, 13, 13, 15) more times.

At the Same Time, Shape Neckline at the End of the Row

(RS) Work in patt to 3 sts before neckline border m, k2tog, k1, sl m, work neckline border sts in patt—1 st dec'd. Work neckline dec every 4 (4, 4, 4, 2, 2, 2) rows 9 (14, 16, 18, 20, 24, 26) more times. 14 (16, 19, 22, 25, 26, 29) sts bet m after all dec complete. Work even in patt until piece measures 7 (7½, 8, 8½, 8¾, 9, 9¼)" (18 [19, 20.5, 21.5, 22, 23, 23.5] cm) from armhole BO, ending after a WS row. BO all sts

except the neckline border sts, work across neckline border sts in patt and place on st holder.

RIGHT FRONT

Put right front held sts on the needle. With WS facing, join yarn.

Next row: (WS) CO 4 sts sleeve border, pm, work in patt to end of row.

Note: Armhole shaping and neckline shaping are worked simultaneously. Read through foll section before proceeding.

Shape Neckline at the Beginning of the Row

(RS) Work neckline border sts, sl m, k1, ssk, work in patt to end of row—1 st dec'd. Work neckline dec every 4 (4, 4, 4, 2, 2, 2) rows 9 (14, 16, 18, 20, 24, 26) more times.

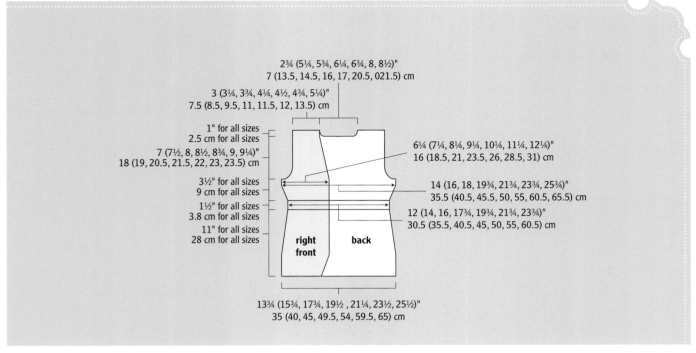

2¾ (5¼, 5¾, 6¼, 6¾, 8, 8½)"
7 (13.5, 14.5, 16, 17, 20.5, 021.5) cm

3 (3¼, 3¾, 4¼, 4½, 4¾, 5¼)"
7.5 (8.5, 9.5, 11, 11.5, 12, 13.5) cm

1" for all sizes
2.5 cm for all sizes

7 (7½, 8, 8½, 8¾, 9, 9¼)"
18 (19, 20.5, 21.5, 22, 23, 23.5) cm

6¼ (7¼, 8¼, 9¼, 10¼, 11¼, 12¼)"
16 (18.5, 21, 23.5, 26, 28.5, 31) cm

3½" for all sizes
9 cm for all sizes

14 (16, 18, 19¾, 21¾, 23¾, 25¾)"
35.5 (40.5, 45.5, 50, 55, 60.5, 65.5) cm

1½" for all sizes
3.8 cm for all sizes

12 (14, 16, 17¾, 19¾, 21¾, 23¾)"
30.5 (35.5, 40.5, 45, 50, 55, 60.5) cm

11" for all sizes
28 cm for all sizes

right front

back

13¾ (15¾, 17¾, 19½ , 21¼, 23½, 25½)"
35 (40, 45, 49.5, 54, 59.5, 65) cm

Van Dyke Border chart to end. Rep the last 2 rows until 9 reps of the Van Dyke Border chart are complete, then work 10 more rows, ending after Row 10 of chart—114 sts total; 5 border sts, 109 shawl sts.

Next row: (RS) Work Van Dyke Border chart to m, sl m, knit to end.

Next row: (WS) Sl 1 st pwise wyf, p1, knit to 2 sts before m, p2, sl m, work Van Dyke Border chart to end. Rep the last 2 rows 9 more times, ending after Row 10 of chart.

Dec row: (RS) Work Van Dyke Border chart to m, sl m, k1, ssk, knit to end—1 shawl st dec'd.

Next row: (WS) Sl 1 st pwise wyf, p1, knit to 2 sts before m, p2, sl m, work in Van Dyke Border chart to end. Rep the last 2 rows until 20 reps of the Van Dyke Border chart are complete, ending after Row 20 of chart—24 sts total; 10 border sts, 14 shawl sts.

Bo Border Sts

(RS) BO 8 sts kwise, sl rem st on right-hand needle to left-hand needle and k2tog, ssk, knit to end—14 sts.

SECOND TAB

Row 1: (WS) Sl 1 st pwise wyf, p1, knit to last 2 sts, p2.

Row 2: Sl 1 st pwise wyb, knit to end.

Rep Rows 1 and 2 until tab measures 8" (20.3 cm) from end of BO of border sts, ending after a WS row.

Shape Tab

Dec row: (RS) Sl 1 st pwise wyb, ssk, knit to last 3 sts, k2tog, k1—2 sts dec'd.

Next row: Sl 1 st pwise wyf, p1, knit to last 2 sts, p2.

Rep the last 2 rows 3 more times, then work dec row once more—4 sts rem. Do not turn work.

SECOND I-CORD

Slide sts back to dpn (with RS facing, working yarn should be attached to the last st worked, hanging off the left side of work). Work I-cord for 14" (35.5 cm).

Dec row: [k2tog] twice—2 sts rem.

Final row: K2tog—1 st rem. Break yarn and draw through rem st.

FINISHING

Weave in ends and block to finished measurements. ✦

CELESTE YOUNG teaches knitting, crocheting, and spinning at Trumpet Hill . . . Fine Yarns & Accents in Albany, New York. She often knits while watching *Lost in Austen,* which is almost as good as reading Jane Austen. She is thrilled to be pursuing level three of the Knitting Guild of America (TKGA) Master Knitting Program. Find her online atcelesteyoungdesigns.com and on Ravelry as celknits.

Van Dyke Border Chart

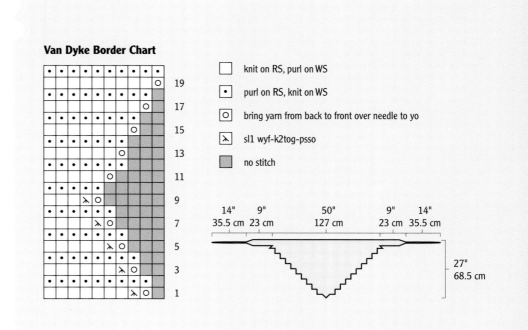

☐ knit on RS, purl on WS

· purl on RS, knit on WS

○ bring yarn from back to front over needle to yo

⅄ sl1 wyf-k2tog-psso

▨ no stitch

14" / 35.5 cm 9" / 23 cm 50" / 127 cm 9" / 23 cm 14" / 35.5 cm

27" / 68.5 cm

Lydia Military Spencer

ANNIE MODESITT

Originally designed as a mockery of the extreme fashions of the Regency period, the spencer jacket became a signature piece of the time and a style Lydia Bennet of *Pride and Prejudice* might have worn. Oddly flattering, simple to wear, and fun to knit up, this jacket will become a perennial favorite in many seasons.

FINISHED SIZE 26¾ (30½, 34¼, 38, 42)" (68 [77.5, 87, 96.5, 106.5] cm) bust circumference. Spencer shown measures 30½".

YARN Worsted weight (#4 Medium) *Shown here:* Brooklyn Tweed Shelter (100% wool; 140 yd [128 m]/50 g): red long johns, 6 (7, 9, 9, 11) skeins.

NEEDLES Size 7 (4.5 mm). Size 8 (5 mm): straight and set of double-pointed (dpn). Size 9 (5.5 mm): straight, 16" (40.5 cm) circular (cir), and set of dpn. Adjust needle sizes if necessary to obtain the correct gauge.

NOTIONS Markers (m); stitch holders; tapestry needle; five ¾" (2 cm) buttons.

GAUGE 21 sts and 24 rows = 4" (10 cm) in herringbone patt on largest needles.

Note

◆ When shaping in the herringbone pattern, do not work a pattern decrease if there are not enough stitches to work its corresponding increase.

BODY

With largest needles, CO 98 (112, 126, 140, 154) sts. Change to middle-size needles. Work 10 rows in St st, ending with a WS row.

Set Up Patt

Change to largest needles. Work Rows 1–6 of Herringbone Setup chart—140 (160, 180, 200, 220) sts. Rep Rows 1 and 2 of 20-st Herringbone chart until piece measures 7¼ (7¾, 8½, 10, 10¼)" (18.5 [19.5, 21.5, 25.5, 26] cm) from top of rolled hem, ending with a WS row.

Divide Fronts and Back

Next row: (RS) Cont in patt as established, work 38 (39, 50, 49, 60) sts, BO 10 (10, 10, 12, 12) sts, work 44 (62, 60, 78, 76) sts, BO 10 (10, 10, 12, 12) sts, work to end—38 (39, 50, 49, 60) sts for each front, 44 (62, 60, 78, 76) sts for back. Break yarn; place front sts on holders.

BACK

With WS facing, rejoin yarn to back sts. Cont in patt as established until armhole measures 8 (8¾, 9½, 9½, 10½)" (20.5 [22, 24, 24, 26.5] cm), ending with a WS row.

Shape Shoulders

Cont in patt as established, BO 4 (5, 5, 6, 7) sts at beg of next 4 rows, then BO 4 (4, 6, 6, 6) sts at beg of foll 2 rows—20 (34, 28, 42, 36) sts rem for back neck. Place sts on holder.

LEFT FRONT

With WS facing, rejoin yarn to left front sts. Cont in patt as established, work even until armhole measures 5¾ (6¼, 6½, 6, 6¾)" (14.5 [16, 16.5, 15, 17] cm), ending with a RS row.

Shape Neck

At beg of WS rows, BO 15 (13, 17, 16, 21) sts once, then BO 2 (2, 4, 3, 4) sts 2 times—19 (22, 25, 27, 31) sts rem. BO 1 st at beg of every WS row 7 (8, 9, 9, 11) times. *At the same time,* when armhole measures 9 (9¾, 10½, 10½, 11½)" (23 [25, 26.5, 26.5, 29] cm), shape shoulder as foll: At beg of RS rows, BO 4 (5, 5, 6, 7) sts 2 times, then BO 4 (4, 6, 6, 6) sts once—no sts rem.

RIGHT FRONT

With WS facing, rejoin yarn to right front sts. Cont in patt as established, work even until armhole measures 5¾ (6¼, 6½, 6, 6¾)" (14.5 [16, 16.5, 15, 17] cm), ending with a WS row.

Shape Neck

At beg of RS rows, BO 15 (13, 17, 16, 21) sts once, then BO 2 (2, 4, 3, 4) sts 2 times—19 (22, 25, 27, 31) sts rem. BO 1 st at beg of every RS row 7 (8, 9, 9, 11) times. *At the same time,* when armhole measures 9 (9¾, 10½, 10½, 11½)" (23 [25, 26.5, 26.5, 29] cm), shape shoulder as foll: At beg of WS rows, BO 4 (5, 5, 6, 7) sts 2 times, then BO 4 (4, 6, 6, 6) sts once—no sts rem. Steam-block pieces. Sew shoulder seams; seams will sit to back of garment.

SLEEVES

With largest cir needle and beg at center of underarm, pick up and knit 72 (78, 84, 84, 96) sts around armhole. Place marker and join in the rnd.

Sleeve Cap

Set-up rnd: Beg with st 1 (1, 4, 4, 4) and ending with st 6, work Row 2 of Sleeve Undercap chart over 12 (12, 15, 15, 15) sts, pm for cap shaping, work Sleeve Cap Setup chart over 24 (27, 27, 27, 33) sts, pm for top of sleeve (this may fall in center of chart), cont Sleeve Cap Setup chart (beg with next st to be worked) over 24 (27, 27, 27, 33) sts, pm for cap shaping, work Row 2 of Sleeve Undercap chart over 12 (12, 15, 15, 15) sts, ending with st 6 (6, 3, 3, 3) of chart—104 (114, 120, 120, 140) sts.

Shape cap using short-rows as foll:

Next row: (RS) Work Row 1 of Sleeve Undercap chart as established over 12 (12, 15, 15, 15) sts, sl m, work Row 1 of Sleeve Cap chart to 1 st before next shaping m, w&t (see Glossary).

Next row: (WS) Work Row 2 of Sleeve Cap chart to 1 st before next shaping m, w&t.

Next row: (RS) Work in patt to 5 sts before last wrapped st, w&t.

Next row: (WS) Work in patt to 5 sts before last wrapped st, w&t. Rep last 2 rows 6 (7, 7, 7, 9) more times—4 sts on each side between last wrapped st and top of sleeve m.

Next row: (RS) Work in patt to top of sleeve m, remove m, cont in patt to shaping m, working wraps tog with wrapped sts as you come to them, sl m, work Row 1 of Sleeve Undercap chart as established to end of rnd.

Next rnd: Work Row 2 of Sleeve Undercap chart as established over 12 (12, 15, 15, 15) sts, sl m, work in patt to m, working wraps tog with wrapped sts as you come to them, sl m, work Row 2 of Sleeve Undercap chart as established to end of rnd.

Next rnd: Work Row 1 of Sleeve Undercap chart as established over 12 (12, 15, 15, 15) sts, remove m, work Sleeve Cap Decrease chart to next m, remove m, work Row 1 of Sleeve Undercap chart as established to end of rnd—72 (78, 84, 84, 96) sts rem.

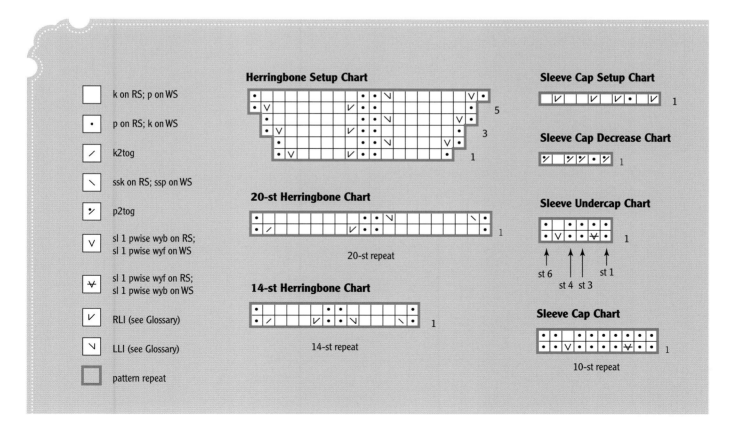

k on RS; p on WS

p on RS; k on WS

k2tog

ssk on RS; ssp on WS

p2tog

sl 1 pwise wyb on RS; sl 1 pwise wyf on WS

sl 1 pwise wyf on RS; sl 1 pwise wyb on WS

RLI (see Glossary)

LLI (see Glossary)

pattern repeat

Herringbone Setup Chart

20-st Herringbone Chart

20-st repeat

14-st Herringbone Chart

14-st repeat

Sleeve Cap Setup Chart

Sleeve Cap Decrease Chart

Sleeve Undercap Chart

st 6   st 1
st 4 st 3

Sleeve Cap Chart

10-st repeat

Lower Sleeve

Next rnd: Purl, dec 2 (8, 0, 0, 12) sts evenly spaced—70 (70, 84, 84, 84) sts rem. Knit 3 rnds.

Next rnd: [P3 (3, 4, 4, 4), p2tog] 14 times—56 (56, 70, 70, 70) sts rem.

Work 14-st Herringbone chart over all sts. Cont in patt until piece measures 18½ (19¼, 20¾, 20¾, 23¼)" (47 [49, 52.5, 52.5, 59] cm) from beg of lower sleeve, or desired length. Change to middle-size dpn. Work 10 rnds in St st. With largest needle, loosely BO all sts.

FINISHING

Left Front Buttonband

With smallest needles and RS facing, pick up and knit 60 (64, 68, 72, 76) sts along left front edge. Work in garter st for 9 rows. With RS facing, loosely BO all sts.

Right Front Buttonhole Band

With smallest needles and RS facing, pick up and knit 60 (64, 68, 72, 76) sts along right front edge. Work in garter st for 2 rows.

Next row: (WS) K3 (5, 5, 5, 5), [BO 2 sts, knit until there are 11 (11, 12, 13, 14) sts on right needle after BO] 4 times, BO 2 sts, knit to end.

Next row: (RS) [Work to BO space, CO 2 sts] 5 times, knit to end. Work in garter st for 5 rows. With largest needle and RS facing, BO all sts.

Collazr

Note: WS of garment is RS of collar.

With smallest needles and WS of garment facing, pick up and knit 5 (5, 6, 5, 4) sts along top of left front band, 33 (38, 40, 37, 38) sts along left front neck edge, k20 (34, 28, 42, 36) from back neck holder, pick up and knit 33 (38, 40, 37, 38) sts along right front neck edge to band, and 5 (5, 6, 5, 4) sts along top of band—96 (120, 120, 126, 120) sts total.

First Short-Row Section

Next row: (WS of collar) P57 (69, 69, 72, 69), w&t.

Next row: (RS) Sl 1, k17, w&t.

Next row: (WS) Sl 1, purl to wrapped st, work wrap tog with wrapped st, p2, w&t.

Next row: (RS) Sl 1, knit to wrapped st, work wrap tog with wrapped st, k2, w&t.

Rep last 2 rows 8 (10, 10, 11, 10) more times—11 (17, 17, 17, 17) sts unworked after last wrap at each end of row.

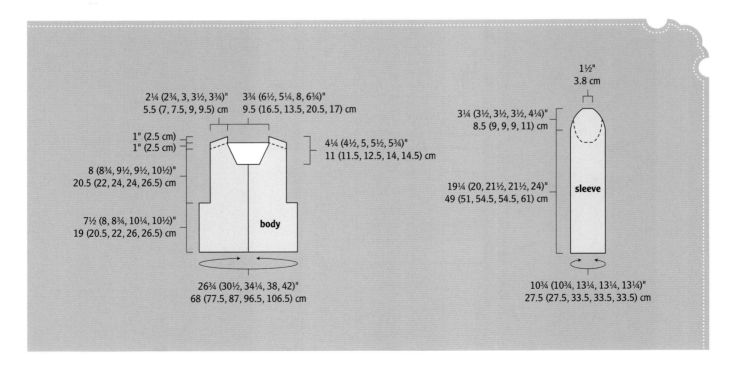

2¼ (2¾, 3, 3½, 3¾)"
5.5 (7, 7.5, 9, 9.5) cm

3¾ (6½, 5¼, 8, 6¾)"
9.5 (16.5, 13.5, 20.5, 17) cm

1" (2.5 cm)
1" (2.5 cm)

4¼ (4½, 5, 5½, 5¾)"
11 (11.5, 12.5, 14, 14.5) cm

8 (8¾, 9½, 9½, 10½)"
20.5 (22, 24, 24, 26.5) cm

7½ (8, 8¾, 10¼, 10½)"
19 (20.5, 22, 26, 26.5) cm

body

26¾ (30½, 34¼, 38, 42)"
68 (77.5, 87, 96.5, 106.5) cm

1½"
3.8 cm

3¼ (3½, 3½, 3½, 4¼)"
8.5 (9, 9, 9, 11) cm

19¼ (20, 21½, 21½, 24)"
49 (51, 54.5, 54.5, 61) cm

sleeve

10¾ (10¾, 13¼, 13¼, 13¼)"
27.5 (27.5, 33.5, 33.5, 33.5) cm

Second Short-Row Section

Change to middle-size needles.

Next row: (WS) Sl 1, purl to wrapped st, work wrap tog with wrapped st, purl to last 8 sts, w&t.

Next row: (RS) Sl 1, knit to wrapped st, work wrap tog with wrapped st, knit to last 8 sts, w&t.

Next row: (WS) Sl 1, purl to 6 sts before wrapped st, w&t.

Next row: (RS) Sl 1, knit to 6 sts before wrapped st, w&t. Rep last 2 rows once more—6 wrapped sts total.

Next row: (WS) Sl 1, purl to end of row, working wraps tog with wrapped sts as you come to them.

Next row: (RS) Knit to end of row, working rem wraps tog with wrapped sts.

Garter Edge

Change to largest needles.

Next row: (WS) Knit to last 8 sts, w&t.

Next row: (RS) Knit to last 8 sts, w&t.

Next row: Knit to wrapped st, work wrap tog with wrapped st, w&t. Rep last row 3 more times—3 wrapped sts at each end.

Next row: Knit to wrapped st, work wrap tog with wrapped st, knit to end. Rep last row once more. With WS facing, loosely BO all sts. Weave in loose ends. ❧

ANNIE MODESITT lives in St. Paul, Minnesota, with her husband, children, pets, and many, many books. She agrees with Miss Austen that "the person, be it gentleman or lady, who has not pleasure in a good novel, must be intolerably stupid."

Summer Pelisse

RENE DICKEY

The romantic effect of layering garments during the Regency era continues to be fashionable and practical today. The pelisse's form—halfway between a coat and a dress—inspired Rene Dickey to create this fanciful cardigan for her daughter to wear over a summer dress. Generous in length and width, the body of the pelisse is knitted in a beautiful, yet easy to learn, lace stitch pattern. The garment is open in the front up to the empire waistline closure, and the design is accentuated by sweet ties where the puffed sleeve caps and waistline are gathered.

FINISHED SIZES 15½ (17, 18, 18¾, 20½)" (39.5 [43, 45.5, 47.5, 52] cm) chest circumference, buttoned with ¼" (6 mm) overlapping buttonband. Shown in 18" (45.5 cm) size.

YARN DK weight (#3 Light)
Shown here: Classic Elite Yarns Wool Bam Boo (50% wool, 50% bamboo; 118 yd [108 m]/50 g): #1691 bay blue, 4 (4, 5, 5, 6) skeins. *(Note: This yarn has been discontinued. Please substitute a DK-weight wool or wool-blend yarn. Always check gauge when substituting yarns.)*

NEEDLES Size 6 (4 mm). Adjust needle size if necessary to obtain correct gauge.

NOTIONS Stitch holder; tapestry needle; Size E/4 (3.5 mm) crochet hook; and three ⅜" (1 cm) buttons.

GAUGE 24 sts and 32 rows = 4" (10 cm) in St st; 23 sts and 32 rows = 4" (10 cm) in Horseshoe Lace.

Note

◆ The body is knitted in one piece to the armholes. The right front, back, and left front are divided and worked separately to the shoulders.

BODY

CO 131 (141, 151, 161, 171) sts. Knit 2 rows. Work Rows 1–8 of Horseshoe Lace chart 7 (7, 8, 8, 9) times.

Dec row: (RS) K5 (10, 10, 5, 10), ★k1, k2tog; rep from ★ , to last (9) sts, 6 (11, 9, 6, 11) sts, knit to end—91 (101, 107, 111, 121) sts.

Next row: (WS) Purl.

Eyelet row: (RS) K0 (2, 0, 3, 0), ★k2, yo, k2tog; rep from ★ to last 3 (3, 3, 4, 1) sts, knit to end-22 (24, 26, 26, 30) eyelets. Work 3 rows in St st, ending with a WS row.

Divide for Right Armhole

Next row: (RS) K23 (25, 27, 28, 30) sts for right front, place rem 68 (76, 80, 83, 91) sts on holder and turn to cont working right front sts only.

RIGHT FRONT

Shape Armhole

Next row: (WS) Cont in St st, BO 2 sts purl to end—21 (23, 25, 26, 28) sts.

Dec row: (RS) Knit to last 2 sts, ssk—1 st dec'd. Rep armhole dec row every RS row 0 (0, 0, 0, 1) more time—20 (22, 24, 25, 26) sts. Cont in St st until armhole measures 1¾ (2, 2½, 2½, 2½)" (4.5 [5, 6.5, 6.5, 6.5] cm) from divide, ending with a WS row.

Shape Neck

Next row: (RS) BO 6 sts knit to end—14 (16, 18, 19, 20) sts.

Next row: (WS) Purl.

Next row: (RS) BO 3 sts, knit to end—11 (13, 15, 16, 17) sts.

Next row: (WS) Purl.

Neck dec row: (RS) K2, ssk, knit to end—1 st dec'd. Rep neck dec row every RS row 3 (3, 4, 4, 4) times—7 (9, 10, 11, 12) sts rem. Cont in St st until armhole measures 3½ (4, 4½, 5, 5½)" (9 [10, 11.5, 12.5, 14] cm) from divide, ending with a WS row. BO rem 7 (9, 10, 11, 12) sts.

BACK

Divide for Back Armholes

Return 45 (51, 53, 55, 61) held back sts to working needle and join yarn preparing to work a RS row. Leave rem 23 (25, 27, 28, 30) sts on the holder for left front.

Shape Armholes

Next row: (RS) Cont in St st, BO 2 sts at beg of next 2 rows—41 (47, 49, 51, 57) sts.

Dec row: (RS) K2tog, knit to last 2 sts, ssk—2 sts dec'd. Rep armhole dec row every RS row 0 (0, 0, 0, 1) time(s)—39 (45, 47, 49, 53) sts. Cont in St st until armholes measure 3 (3½, 4, 4½, 5)" (7.5 [9, 10, 11.5, 12.5] cm) from divide, ending with a WS row.

Shape Back Neck

Next row: (RS) K8 (10, 11, 12, 13) sts, BO center 23 (25, 25, 25, 27) sts and knit to end.

Left Shoulder

Next row: (WS) Purl to neck opening and turn.

Left neck dec row: (RS) K2tog, knit to end—7 (9, 10, 11, 12) sts. BO rem left shoulder sts.

Right Shoulder

With WS facing, join yarn at other side of neck, and purl across.

Right neck dec row: (RS) Knit to last 2 sts, ssk—7 (9, 10, 11, 12) sts. BO rem right shoulder sts.

LEFT FRONT

Return 23 (25, 27, 28, 30) held left front sts to working needle and join yarn preparing to work a RS row.

Shape Armhole

(RS) Cont in St st, BO 2 sts, knit to end—21 (23, 25, 26, 28) sts.

Next row: (WS) Purl.

Dec row: (RS) K2tog, knit to end—1 st dec'd. Rep armhole dec row every RS row 0 (0, 0, 0, 1) time(s)—20 (22, 24, 25, 26) sts. Cont in St st until armhole measures 1¾ (2, 2½, 2½, 2½)" (4.5 [5, 6.5, 6.5, 6.5] cm) from divide, ending with a RS row.

Shape Neck

(WS) BO 6 sts, purl to end—14 (16, 18, 19, 20) sts.

Next row: (RS) Knit.

Next row: (WS) BO 3 sts, purl to end—11 (13, 15, 16, 17) sts.

Neck dec row: (RS) Knit to last 4 sts, k2tog, k2—1 st dec'd. Rep neck dec row every RS row 3 (3, 4, 4, 4) times—7 (9, 10, 11, 12) sts. Cont in St st until armhole 3½ (4, 4½, 5, 5½)" (9 [10, 11.5, 12.5, 14] cm) from divide, ending with a RS row. BO 7 (9, 10, 11, 12) sts.

Horseshoe Lace Chart

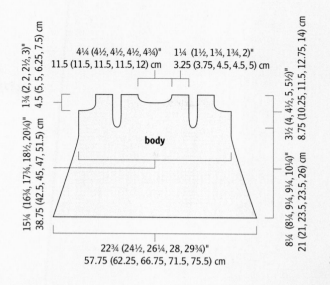

knit on RS, purl on WS

• purl on RS, knit on WS

o yo

↗ sl 1-k2tog-psso

pattern repeat

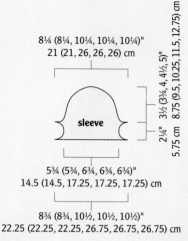

SLEEVES

CO 51 (51, 61, 61, 61) sts. Knit 2 rows. Work Rows 1–8 of Horseshoe Lace chart.

Dec row: (RS) *K1, k2tog; rep from * to last 0 (0, 1, 1, 1) st(s), knit to end—34 (34, 41, 41, 41) sts rem.

Next row: (WS) Purl.

Eyelet row: *K2, yo, k2tog; rep from * to last 2 (2, 1, 1, 1) st(s), knit to end—8 (8, 10, 10, 10) eyelets. Cont in St st for 3 rows, ending with a WS row.

Inc row: *K2, M1 rep from * to last 2 (2, 1, 1, 1) sts, knit to end—50 (50, 61, 61, 61) sts.

Next row: (WS) Purl.

Shape Cap

(RS) Cont in St st, BO 2 sts at beg of next 2 rows—46 (46, 57, 57, 57) sts rem.

Cap dec row: (RS) K2tog, knit to last 2 sts, ssk—2 sts dec'd. Rep Cap Dec Row every RS row 0 (0, 0, 0, 1) time(s)—44 (44, 55, 55, 53) sts. Cont in St st for 23 (25, 27, 31, 33) rows, ending with a WS row.

Dec row 1: (RS) K1 (1, 2, 2, 1), [sssk] 7 (7, 8, 8, 8) times, [k3tog] 7 (7, 9, 9, 9) times, k1 (1, 2, 2, 1)—16 (16, 21, 21, 19) sts.

Dec row 2: (WS) P1, [p2tog] 7 (7, 9, 9, 8) times, p1 (1, 2, 2, 2)—9 (9, 12, 12, 11) sts. BO all sts.

FINISHING

Block pieces to measurements. Sew shoulder seams. Sew sleeves into armholes. Sew sleeve seams.

Buttonband

With RS facing, pick up and knit 62 (66, 72, 76, 86) sts evenly along left front edge.

Next row: (WS) Knit. BO all sts kwise. Mark placement of 3 buttons, one just below the neck, one ½" (1.3 cm) above Eyelet Row on body, and the third spaced evenly between.

Buttonhole Band

With RS facing, pick up and knit 62 (66, 72, 76, 86) sts evenly along right front edge.

Buttonhole row: (WS) *Knit until you reach button m, yo, k2tog; rep from * 2 times, knit to end. BO all sts kwise.

Neckband

With RS facing, pick up and knit 54 (60, 60, 66, 74) sts evenly around neck opening. Knit 3 rows. BO all sts kwise.

Sleeve Ties (make 2)

With crochet hook, ch for 18" (45.5 cm) and fasten off.

Body Tie

With crochet hook, ch for 34 (36, 38, 40, 42)" (86.5 [91.5, 96.5, 101.5, 106.5] cm) and fasten off. Weave ties through the yo's in each Eyelet Row and tie with a bow. Weave in all loose ends, sew on buttons securely, and block again, if desired. ❧

RENE DICKEY has worked and taught at a couple of local yarn shops; finished a ton of sweaters with her business, Knits Finished; and is now super excited to be focusing on her knitwear designs. She lives in beautiful Snoqualmie, Washington, with her daughter and husband. See more of her work at cascadiaknitwear.com or as ReneD on Ravelry.

Hetty's Sunday Cuffs

DANELLE SORENSEN

Poor Hetty Bates! As we know, from Mr. Knightley's lecture to Emma, "She is poor; she has sunk from the comforts she was born to; and, if she live to old age, must probably sink more." These cuffs are just the sort of project sure to be treasured by Miss Bates herself—a precious smidgen of luxurious fiber intended to dress up the ordinary, common clothes of the workday week. Simple lace patterns, knitted in the round, become the perfect showcase for a wool/silk blend with lovely drape and sheen.

FINISHED SIZES 6½" (16.5 cm) circumference and 6¼" (16 cm) long.

YARN Fingering weight (# Super fine) *Shown here:* Spud & Chloë Fine (80% superwash wool, 20% silk; 248 yd [227 m]/65 g): #7816 dragonfly, one skein. Distributed by Blue Sky Alpacas.

NEEDLES Size 1 (2.25 mm) double-pointed (dpn). Adjust needle size if necessary to obtain the correct gauge.

GAUGE 30 sts and 32 rnds = 4" (10 cm) in St st.

Notes

- *The cuff consists of four parts: a Folded Picot Hem; a plain stockinette section; a section of lace alternating with stockinette; and, finally, a solid lace edge. You may customize the length of the cuffs by adjusting the **number of rounds** in any section. Adjustments may require more yardage.*

- *The lace stitch patterns consist of a one-round pattern alternating with a round of plain knitting—very rhythmic and easy to memorize.*

- *Most 3-ply fingering-weight yarns will work, however wool blended with silk will result in a fabric that hugs the wrist while allowing the lace stitches to shine. Choose a yarn suitable for wet-blocking to maximize the delicate lace patterns.*

- *These cuffs are versatile and can be worn with either the hem or the lace edge around the palm—you decide!*

Stitch Guide

ALTERNATING LACE

Rnd 1: *K6, yo, k1, sl 1 kwise wyb, k2tog, psso, k1, yo, k1*; rep from * to end.

Rnd 2: Knit.

Rep Rnds 1–2 for pattern.

SOLID LACE

Rnd 1: *Yo, k1, sl 1 kwise wyb, k2tog, psso, k1, yo, k1*; rep from * to end.

Rnd 2: Knit.

Rep Rnds 1–2 for pattern.

CUFFS

Using the Long-tail method (see Glossary), CO 48 sts. Pm for beg of rnd and join for working in the rnd. Work Folded Picot Hem as foll: Knit 9 rnds.

Picot turning rnd: ★Yo, k2tog; rep from ★ to end. Knit 9 more rnds. This completes the hem and will be handsewn later. Knit an additional 20 rnds. Work Alternating Lace patt for 10 rnds. Work Solid Lace patt for 10 rnds. BO all sts very loosely, this edge will be stretched during blocking.

FINISHING

Turn Picot Hem to WS along turning rnd and sew in place. Do not weave ends until after blocking. Wet-block, pulling out points on lace edge and each picot on the folded hem. Weave in all loose ends. ❧

DANELLE SORENSEN dodges tornadoes in Kansas, teaches kindergarten through twelfth grade in a very private school, and never turns down an opportunity to enjoy afternoon tea. Prior to the advent of digital books, she actually wore out a hard copy of *Pride and Prejudice*. Find Danelle on Ravelry as AuntDaniKnits.

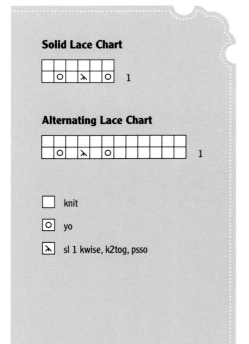

Solid Lace Chart

| | o | | ⋏ | | o | | 1 |

Alternating Lace Chart

| | o | | ⋏ | | o | | | | | | 1 |

☐	knit
o	yo
⋏	sl 1 kwise, k2tog, psso

JANE AUSTEN, *Multitasker*

BY REBECCA DICKSON

Jane Austen was born on the same day as Ludwig van Beethoven, though five years later. When Beethoven was born, in 1770, he wasn't expected to become accomplished at many different tasks. It would be acceptable if he became, say, merely a fine pianist and composer. But when baby Jane was born on December 16, 1775, there were widely different expectations of her, all of which she would meet. Among other things, she would become an accomplished pianist, though perhaps she wasn't quite as able as Ludwig.

Understanding the different expectations of boys and girls in the late eighteenth century helps to convey the nature of Austen's culture and the difficulties a woman faced in becoming a respected writer. It also helps explain how uniquely gifted Jane Austen was.

Unlike Beethoven, Austen was an accomplished needleworker. This was expected of her—any middle-class woman of the eighteenth and early nineteenth centuries was expected to be able to create things with her hands. For working- and middle-class women, it was necessary work. They made their own clothes and their family's clothes, they darned socks, and they made household furnishings and decorations. While a middle-class man could spend his time being good at one thing, women weren't encouraged to focus on a single activity; they needed many skills and abilities to win a husband and help run a household. Even if, like Austen, a woman did not marry, she needed to be an able worker—she needed to be able to cook, sew, do needlework, keep a garden, and supervise servants who did the heavy work.

Women were also expected to be the entertainers of the household—they were expected to sing, dance, draw, and recite poetry. When she was a teenager, Austen read aloud her

BENJAMIN S. CLARKE

own early works to her family, who were very supportive of her writing. When she was older, Austen played the piano for her nieces and nephews and houseguests so they could all dance. Her nephew James Edward Austen-Leigh describes her as being "successful in everything that she attempted with her fingers." She made lace and fashioned little handkerchiefs. She and her sister and mother made a patchwork quilt that can still be viewed at her home in Chawton. Was Jane Austen a knitter? That's not clear, but she likely was, as most women in England at that time and of Austen's social standing and situation were knitters.

What is clear is that Jane Austen knew how to work—she had a determined self-discipline that is as inspiring as her novels themselves. She was happy enough for others to know of her typical employments, but she didn't want any attention drawn to her writing. She didn't want anyone besides her closest confidantes to know how seriously she took her writing. James Edward tells us that she wouldn't allow the maid to grease the door into the sitting room because she wanted to hear if someone was coming into the room so she could hide her latest writing project.

Why? Because in Austen's world, men were expected to be the good writers. In 1800, a woman was considered audacious if she tried to do something more than piecework, housework, and entertaining. Jane Austen was quietly pretty audacious.

Encouraged and supported in his work, Beethoven gave the world *Ode to Joy*, while Austen, with the aid of squeaky hinges, discreetly penned Elizabeth Bennet and never once neglected her needlework. ❧

REBECCA DICKSON teaches writing and rhetoric at the University of Colorado at Boulder. The author of *Jane Austen: An Illustrated Treasury* (Storey, 2008), she lives in Boulder, Colorado, with two cats and her husband.

Georgiana Darcy's Fancy Shawl

KAREN JOAN RAZ

Georgiana Darcy of *Pride and Prejudice* was a lovely young woman just on the brink of adulthood—at an age when she would be preparing to attend her first ball. Along with a beautiful gown, what could be more appropriate than a demure lacy wrap edged with tiny pearls? The body of this rectangular wrap uses a provisional cast-on, then a fancy bind-off with tiny pearls is worked the same on both ends. The pearls are added using the crochet-hook method.

FINISHED SIZE About 20" (51 cm) wide and 76" (193 cm) long, after blocking.

YARN Lace weight (#0 Lace)
Shown here: Claudia Hand Painted Yarns Silk Lace (100% silk; 1,100 yd [1,006 m]/3½ oz [100 g]), navy olive, 1 skein.

NEEDLES Size 6 (4 mm). Adjust needle size if necessary to obtain the correct gauge.

NOTIONS Tapestry needle; 240 size 8.0 round glass seed beads (shown here: Toho Ceylon light ivory); size 13 (0.85 mm) steel crochet hook, or size to fit holes in beads.

GAUGE 20½ sts and 22 rows = 4" (10 cm) in lace patt from Body chart, after blocking (see Note); 20 to 24 sts of Border chart measure about 6" (15 cm) at widest point.

Note

◆ As with all lace shawls, gauge is approximate and not as important as producing a satisfying drape and hand.

Stitch Guide

ADD BEAD: Place 1 bead on shank of crochet hook. Sl the next st on left needle onto the hook and hold it taut. Slide the bead down onto the st, then return the beaded st to the left needle and work it as k1.

BODY

Using a provisional method, CO 103 sts.

Set-up row 1: (RS) Knit.

Set-up row 2: (WS) K2, p99, k2.

Work Rows 1–24 of Body chart 14 times, then work Rows 1–13 once more, ending with a RS row—349 chart rows completed.

Next row: (WS) K1, k1f&b, p99, k1f&b, k1—105 sts. Do not break yarn.

FIRST BORDER

With RS facing, use the cable method to CO 20 sts onto left needle for border.

Set-up row 1: (RS) K17, ssk, yo, ssk (last border st tog with 1 body st after it), turn—20 border sts; 1 body st has been joined.

Set-up row 2: (WS) Sl 1 pwise, p17, add bead to next st (see Stitch Guide), k1, turn.

Work Rows 1–10 of Border chart 20 times, then work Rows 1–8 once more, joining the last border st tog with 1 body st at the end of each RS row—24 border sts; no body sts rem. BO all sts. Break yarn.

SECOND BORDER

With WS of body facing, place 103 sts from provisional CO on needle and rejoin yarn.

Next row: (WS) K1, k1f&b, p99, k1f&b, k1—105 sts.

Work Border chart as for first border until all body sts have been joined. BO rem 24 border sts.

FINISHING

Weave in ends. Wet-block to measurements. ✤

KAREN JOAN RAZ is a freelance designer from Bolingbrook, Illinois, specializing in beaded lace shawls. On Ravelry, her username is laceknit.

Body Chart

23 21 19 17 15 13 11 9 7 5 3 1

13 st repeat
work 2 times

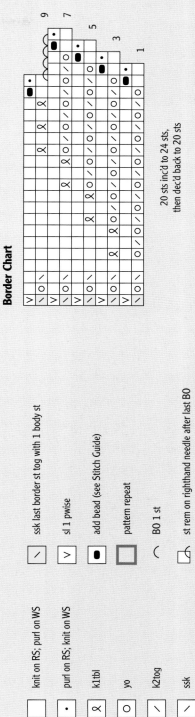

Border Chart

9 7 5 3 1

20 sts inc'd to 24 sts,
then dec'd back to 20 sts

	knit on RS; purl on WS		/	ssk last border st tog with 1 body st
•	purl on RS; knit on WS		>	sl 1 pwise
⋉	k1tbl		●	add bead (see Stitch Guide)
O	yo		▢	pattern repeat
\	k2tog		⌒	BO 1 st
/	ssk		⌐	st rem on righthand needle after last BO

Diamonds and Crosses Border Chart

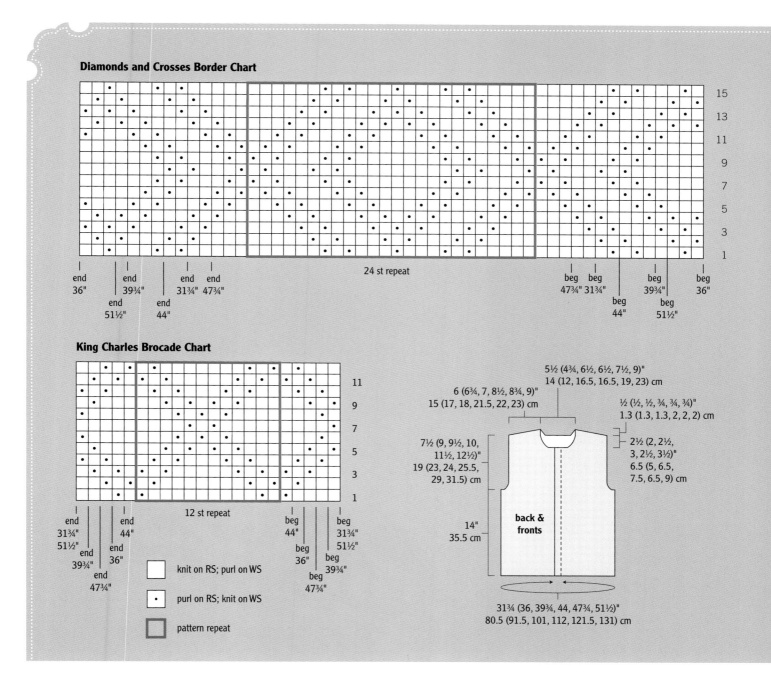

15
13
11
9
7
5
3
1

24 st repeat

end 36"
end 39¾"
end 31¾" end 47¾"
end 51½"
end 44"

beg 47¾" beg 31¾"
beg 39¾"
beg 36"
beg 44"
beg 51½"

King Charles Brocade Chart

11
9
7
5
3
1

12 st repeat

end 31¾" 51½"
end 44"
end 39¾"
end 36"
end 47¾"

beg 44"
beg 31¾" 51½"
beg 36"
beg 39¾"
beg 47¾"

□ knit on RS; purl on WS

▪ purl on RS; knit on WS

▢ pattern repeat

5½ (4¾, 6½, 6½, 7½, 9)"
14 (12, 16.5, 16.5, 19, 23) cm

6 (6¾, 7, 8½, 8¾, 9)"
15 (17, 18, 21.5, 22, 23) cm

½ (½, ½, ¾, ¾, ¾)"
1.3 (1.3, 1.3, 2, 2, 2) cm

7½ (9, 9½, 10, 11½, 12½)"
19 (23, 24, 25.5, 29, 31.5) cm

2½ (2, 2½, 3, 2½, 3½)"
6.5 (5, 6.5, 7.5, 6.5, 9) cm

14"
35.5 cm

back & fronts

31¾ (36, 39¾, 44, 47¾, 51½)"
80.5 (91.5, 101, 112, 121.5, 131) cm

With yarn threaded on a tapestry nee-dle, sew buttons on top of buttonholes to close them, placing buttons on right front for a man's vest or on left front for a woman's vest (see Notes). ✤

KATHLEEN DAMES designs and knits in New York City and Bath, Maine, with her very own Captain Wentworth and their three children. All of Jane Austen's works have provided her with joy and inspiration. You can find more of Kathleen's designs at kathleendames.blogspot.com, and she goes by the username Purly on Ravelry.

Damask Mittens

MARIA YARLEY

As a lover of all things Austen, Maria Yarley has enjoyed the rise in popularity of damask over the last few years. There is something so lovely about seeing Regency-inspired prints grace everything from windows and sofas to the covers of journals and photo albums. The extensive variety of beautiful Regency fabric prints and the range of these intricate and feminine fabric prints was a large part of the inspiration for the colorwork designs for these mittens.

FINISHED SIZE About 6½" (16.5 cm) hand circumference and 8½" (21.5 cm) long from CO edge to tip of fingers. To fit a child (see Notes).

YARN Fingering weight (#1 Super Fine)
Shown here: Brown Sheep Company Nature Spun Fingering (100% wool; CO 310 yd [283 m]/1¾ oz [50 g]): #N91 Aran (MC), 1 skein; #146 pomegranate (CC), 1 skein.

NEEDLES Size 00 (1.75 mm): set of 4 or 5 double-pointed (dpn). Adjust needle size if necessary to obtain the correct gauge.

NOTIONS Markers (m); tapestry needle; waste yarn.

GAUGE 55 sts and 55 rnds = 4" (10 cm) in St st colorwork patts from charts.

Notes

◆ The gauge of this project is deliberately tighter than the gauge recommended on the yarn label.

◆ The mittens may also be worked on two circular needles, or on one circular needle using the magic loop method.

◆ This project is planned for an exact number of stitches and rounds, so the only option for adjusting size is to change the gauge. For larger mittens, work at a looser gauge on larger needles. Every 4 stitches and 4 rounds fewer in 4 inches (i.e., 51 sts and 51 rnds = 4" [10 cm], or 47 sts and 47 rnds = 4") will increase the hand circumference by about ½", and increase the overall length by about ½". Work a generous swatch in one of the chart patterns to determine your new gauge and evaluate whether you like the resulting fabric.

CUFF

With CC and using the long-tail method, CO 112 sts, Join for working in the rnd, being careful not to twist sts.

Work braid patt as foll:

Rnd 1: ★K1 MC, k1 CC; rep from ★ to end.

Rnd 2: ★With both yarns in front, bring MC under CC and p1 MC, then bring CC under MC and p1 CC; rep from ★ to end.

Note: The yarns will become twisted, but the next rnd will untwist them.

Rnd 3: With both yarns in front, bring MC over CC and p1 MC, then bring CC over MC and p1 CC; rep from ★ to end.

Work Rnds 1–26 of Cuff chart, dec in Rnds 12, 24, and 26 as shown—80 sts.

Work Rnds 1–3 of braid patt as for start of cuff once more—piece measures 2¼" (5.5 cm) from CO. Place sts on holder and set aside. Work second cuff in the same manner, but leave sts on the needles.

RIGHT HAND

Set-up rnd: Work Rnd 1 of Back chart over 44 sts inc 1 st as shown, place marker (pm), work Rnd 1 of Right Palm chart over 36 sts—81 sts. Rnd begins at little finger side of hand, at start of back-of-hand sts.

Thumb Gusset

Work Rnds 2–24 of charts as established, inc for thumb gusset as shown on palm chart—89 sts total; 45 back sts and 44 palm sts. Work even as established until Rnd 31 of charts has been completed.

	St st with MC		R	M1R with color indicated
◆	St st with CC		+	pick up and knit 1 st with MC
╱	k2tog with color indicated			no stitch
╲	ssk with color indicated			pattern repeat
L	M1L with color indicated			

Cuff Chart

25 23 21 19 17 15 13 11 9 7 5 3 1

28 st repeat dec'd to 20 st repeat
work 4 times

Thumb Chart

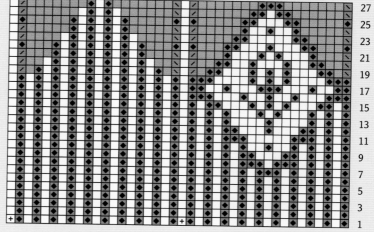

27 25 23 21 19 17 15 13 11 9 7 5 3 1

38 sts inc'd to 40 sts, then dec'd to 12 sts

Back Chart

85
83
81
79
77
75
73
71
69
67
65
63
61
59
57
55
53
51
49
47
45
43
41
39
37
35
33
31
29
27
25
23
21
19
17
15
13
11
9
7
5
3
1

44 sts inc'd to 45 sts, then dec'd to 7 sts

Next rnd: (thumb position; Rnd 32 of charts) Work 45 back sts in patt, work first 2 palm sts, knit the next 19 sts with waste yarn, return the waste yarn sts to the left needle and work these 19 sts again in chart patt (outlined in blue), then work in patt to end of rnd.

Upper Hand

Work Rnds 33–66 of charts as established—piece measures 7" (18 cm) from CO.

Shape Tip

Work Rnds 67–85 of charts, dec as shown—13 sts rem; piece measures 8½" (21.5 cm) from CO. Arrange sts on 2 dpn with 7 Back chart sts on one needle and 6 Right Palm chart sts on the other. Break yarns, leaving a long tail of CC for grafting. Using Kitchener st and CC threaded on a tapestry needle, graft tip of mitten closed, joining 2 back sts to 1 palm st near the center of the tip to accommodate the 1-st difference.

LEFT HAND

Return 80 held sts of second cuff to needles and rejoin yarns.

Set-up rnd: Work Rnd 1 of Back chart over 44 sts inc 1 st as shown, pm, work Rnd 1 of Left Palm chart over 36 sts—81 sts. Rnd begins at thumb side of hand, at start of back-of-hand sts.

Thumb Gusset

Work Rnds 2–24 of charts as established, inc for thumb gusset as shown on palm chart—89 sts total; 45 back sts and 44 palm sts. Work even as established until Rnd 31 of charts has been completed.

Next rnd: (thumb position; Rnd 32 of charts) Work 45 back sts in patt, work first 24 palm sts in patt, knit the next 19 sts with waste yarn, return the waste yarn sts to the left needle and work these 19 sts again in chart patt (outlined in blue), then work last palm st.

Upper Hand

Work Rnds 33–66 of charts as established—piece measures 7" (18 cm) from CO.

Shape Tip

Work Rnds 67–85 of charts, dec as shown—13 sts rem; piece measures 8½" (21.5 cm) from CO. Close tip of mitten as for right hand.

THUMB

With the palm side of the mitten facing you, carefully remove the waste yarn marking the thumb position, and place 19 exposed live sts from the bottom of the thumb opening on one needle, and 19 loops from the top of the thumb opening on a separate needle—38 sts. Join yarns to beg of sts on bottom needle.

Next rnd: Work first 19 sts from Rnd 1 of Thumb chart across 19 sts from bottom of opening, pick up and knit 1 st with MC between needles as shown on chart, work next 19 sts of chart across sts from top of opening, then pick up and knit 1 st with MC between needles as shown—40 sts.

Rearrange sts as evenly as possible on 3 or 4 dpn. Work Rnds 2–18 of chart—thumb measures about 1¼" (3.2 cm).

Shape Tip

Work Rnds 19–27 of charts, dec as shown—12 sts; thumb measures about 2" (5 cm). Arrange sts on 2 dpn with 6 sts on each needle. Break yarns, leaving a long

Left Palm Chart

36 sts inc'd to 44 sts, then dec'd to 6 sts

Right Palm Chart

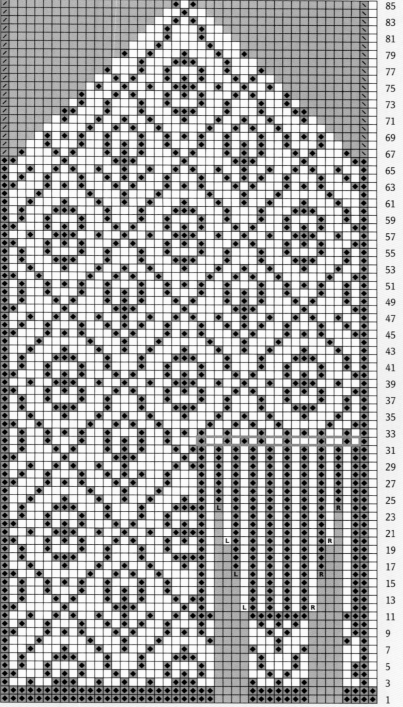

85
83
81
79
77
75
73
71
69
67
65
63
61
59
57
55
53
51
49
47
45
43
41
39
37
35
33
31
29
27
25
23
21
19
17
15
13
11
9
7
5
3
1

36 sts inc'd to 44 sts, then dec'd to 6 sts

tail of CC for grafting. Use Kitchener st and CC threaded on a tapestry needle to graft tip of thumb closed. Work the thumb of the other mitten in the same manner.

FINISHING

Weave in ends using yarn tails to close up any gaps at base of thumbs. Block. ✽

MARIA YARLEY has recently settled in the North Carolina countryside. Since designing her first pair of mittens twenty years ago, Maria has found her niche in exploring knitted textures and translating bold prints into trendy colorwork stitch patterns. You can keep up with what she is working on at eleganteconomydesigns.com and facebook.com/eleganteconomy.

Boteh Shawl

LISA JACOBS

In Jane Austen's day, warm rectangular shawls and wraps complemented filmy Regency dresses, and among the most popular designs was the Paisley shawl. The pattern was woven in Paisley, Scotland, with modified looms that could produce textiles with up to five colors, simulating the colorful hand embroidery of the *boteh* shape (now called Paisley) on shawls from Kasmir and India. Reinterpreted into lace knitting, the Boteh Shawl showcases Regency style for a modern age. Texture replaces color, using an innovative combination of lace and cables that allows each motif to stand out plainly against the reverse stockinette background. Like most Regency Paisley shawls, this elegant wrap features patterned panels at both ends and a plain center.

FINISHED SIZE 14½" (37 cm) wide and 75" (190.5 cm) long, relaxed after blocking.

YARN Lace weight (#0 Lace)
Shown here: Malabrigo Lace (100% Merino; 470 yd [430m]/1¾ oz [50 g]): #123 Rhodesian, 3 skeins.

NEEDLES Size 6 (4 mm): 24" (60 cm) circular (cir) or straight. Adjust needle size if necessary to obtain the correct gauge.

NOTIONS Markers (m); cable needle (cn); tapestry needle.

GAUGE 27 sts and 36 rows = 4" (10 cm) in St st, relaxed after blocking; 36 to 44 sts of paisley charts measure about 5¼" (13.5 cm) wide, relaxed after blocking.

FIRST PAISLEY PANEL

CO 98 sts. Knit 20 rows, ending with a WS row.

Eyelet row: (RS) K8, ssk, yo, place marker (pm), [p2tog, yo] 39 times, sl m, k10—78 center sts between m, 10 border sts each side.

Next row: (WS) Knit, slipping markers (sl m) as you come to them.

Next row: (RS) K8, ssk, yo, sl m, p78, sl m, yo, k2tog, k8.

Rep the last 2 rows 3 more times, ending with a RS row—8 rows completed above eyelet row.

Chart A Section

Set-up row: (WS) K10, sl m, k3, pm, ★work Set-up row of Chart A over 36 sts, inc them to 40 sts as shown, pm; rep from ★ once more, k3, sl m, k10—106 sts; 80 center sts between m, 10 border sts each side.

Next row: (RS) K8, ssk, yo, sl m, p3, sl m, ★work Row 1 of Chart A over 40 sts, sl m; rep from ★ once more, sl m, p3, sl m, yo k2tog, k8.

Working 10 border sts at each side as established in the last 2 rows, and working 3 sts next to each border in rev St st (purl on RS, knit on WS), work Rows 2–72 of chart, ending with a WS row.

Next row: (RS) K8, ssk, yo, sl m, p3, remove m, ★work Row 73 of Chart A, remove m; rep from ★ once more, p3, sl m, yo, k2tog, k8—98 sts; 78 center sts between m, 10 border sts each side.

Chart B Section

Set-up row: (WS) K10, sl m, k21, pm, work Set-up row of Chart B over 36 sts, inc them to 40 sts as shown, pm, k21, sl m, k10—102 sts: 40 center sts in chart patt, 21 rev St sts each side of chart, 10 border sts each side.

Next row: (RS) K8, ssk, yo, sl m, p21, sl m, work Row 1 of Chart B over 40 sts, sl m, p21, sl m, yo, k2tog, k8.

Working 10 border sts at each side as established and sts surrounding chart section in rev St st, work Rows 2–72 of chart, ending with a WS row.

Next row: (RS) K8, ssk, yo, sl m, p21, remove m, work Row 73 of Chart B, remove m, p21, sl m, yo, k2tog, k8—98 sts; 78 center sts between m, 10 border sts each side.

Chart A Section

Work as for first Chart A section, ending with RS Row 73 of chart—98 sts; 78 center sts between m, 10 border sts each side.

Next row: (WS) Knit.

Next row: (RS) K8, ssk, yo, sl m, p78, sl m, yo, k2tog, k8.

Rep the last 2 rows 2 more times, then work 1 more WS row—7 rows completed after last row of chart.

Eyelet row: (RS) K8, ssk, yo, sl m, [p2tog, yo] 39 times, sl m, k10.

Leaving side m in place, knit 13 rows, ending with WS row.

CENTER PANEL

Row 1: (RS, eyelet row) K8, ssk, yo, sl m, [k2tog, yo] 39 times, sl m, k10.

Row 2: (WS) K10, sl m, p78, sl m, k10.

Row 3: K8, ssk, yo, sl m, k78, sl m, yo, k2tog, k8.

Rows 4–150: Rep Rows 2 and 3 seventy-three more times, then work WS Row 2 once more.

Row 151: Rep Row 1 (eyelet row).

SECOND PAISLEY PANEL

Leaving side m in place, knit 13 rows, beg and ending with a WS row.

Eyelet row: (RS) K8, ssk, yo, sl m, [p2tog, yo] 39 times, sl m, k10.

Next row: (WS) Knit, sl m as you come to them.

Next row: (RS) K8, ssk, yo, sl m, p78, sl m, yo, k2tog, k8.

Rep the last 2 rows 3 more times, ending with a RS row—8 rows completed above eyelet row.

Chart B Section

Set-up row: (WS) K10, sl m, k3, pm, ★work Set-up row of Chart B over 36 sts, inc them to 40 sts as shown, pm; rep from ★ once more, k3, sl m, k10—106 sts: 80 center sts between m, 10 border sts each side.

Next row: (RS) K8, ssk, yo, sl m, p3, sl m, ★work Row 1 of Chart B over 40 sts, sl m; rep from ★ once more, sl m, p3, sl m, yo k2tog, k8.

Working 10 border sts at each side as established in the last 2 rows, and working 3 sts next to each border in rev St st, work Rows 2–72 of chart, ending with a WS row.

Next row: (RS) K8, ssk, yo, sl m, p3, remove m, ★work Row 73 of Chart B, remove m; rep from ★ once more, p3, sl m, yo, k2tog, k8—98 sts: 78 center sts between m, 10 border sts each side.

Chart A Section

Set-up row: (WS) K10, sl m, k21, pm, work Set-up row of Chart A over 36 sts, inc them to 40 sts as shown, pm, k21, sl m, k10—102 sts; 40 center sts in chart patt, 21 rev St sts each side of chart, 10 border sts each side.

Next row: (RS) K8, ssk, yo, sl m, p21, sl m, work Row 1 of Chart A over 40 sts, sl m, p21, sl m, yo, k2tog, k8.

Working 10 border sts at each side as established and sts surrounding chart section in rev St st, work Rows 2–72 of chart, ending with a WS row.

Next row: (RS) K8, ssk, yo, sl m, p21, remove m, work Row 73 of Chart A, remove m, p21, sl m, yo, k2tog, k8—98 sts; 78 center sts between m, 10 border sts each side.

Chart B Section
Work as for first Chart B section in this panel, ending with RS Row 73 of

chart—98 sts; 78 center sts between m, 10 border sts each side.

Next row: (WS) Knit.

Next row: (RS) K8, ssk, yo, sl m, p78, sl m, yo, k2tog, k8.

Rep the last 2 rows 2 more times, then work 1 more WS row—7 rows completed after last row of chart.

Eyelet row: (RS) K8, ssk, yo, sl m, [p2tog, yo] 39 times, sl m, k10.

Removing side m as you come to them, knit 20 rows, ending with RS row. Loosely BO all sts.

FINISHING
Weave in ends. Block to a few inches larger than 14½" (37 cm) wide and 75" (190.5 cm) long (piece will relax after blocking). ✤

LISA JACOBS designs nature-inspired patterns for Fiber Tree Designs in Nether Providence, Pennsylvania.

☐	knit on RS; purl on WS
☐	purl on RS; knit on WS
O	yo
/	k2tog
\	ssk on RS; ssp on WS
⟍	p2tog
⟍	ssp
⟋	p3tog on RS; k3tog on WS
⟍	k3tog tbl on WS
M	M1 on WS
L	M1L pwise
R	M1R pwise
V	sl 1 pwise wyb on RS, wyf on WS
▨	no stitch
⌣	k1f&b on WS
⧄	sl 1 st onto cn, hold in back, k1, k1 from cn
⧄	sl 1 st onto cn, hold in front, k1, k1 from cn
⧄	sl 1 st onto cn, hold in back, p1, k1 from cn
⧄	sl 1 st onto cn, hold in front, p1, k1 from cn
⧄	sl 1 st onto cn, hold in front, p2, k1 from cn
⧄	sl 1 st onto cn, hold in back, k2, p1 from cn
⧄	sl 2 sts onto cn, hold in front, k2, p1 from cn
⧄	sl 2 sts onto cn, hold in back, k2, k2 from cn
⧄	RS: sl 2 sts onto cn, hold in front, k2, k2 from cn WS: sl 2 sts onto cn, hold in front, p2, p2 from cn
⧄	RS and WS: sl 2 sts onto cn, hold in back, k2, p2 from cn
⧄	RS and WS: sl 2 sts onto cn, hold in front, p2, k2 from cn
⧄	sl 3 sts onto cn, hold in back, k2, p3 from cn
⧄	RS: sl 2 sts onto cn, hold in front, p3, k2 from cn WS: sl 3 sts onto cn, hold on front, p2, k3 from cn
⧄	sl 4 sts onto cn, hold in back, k2, p4 from cn
⧄	sl 2 sts onto cn, hold in front, p4, k2 from cn
⧄	sl 2 sts onto cn, hold in front, p5, k2 from cn

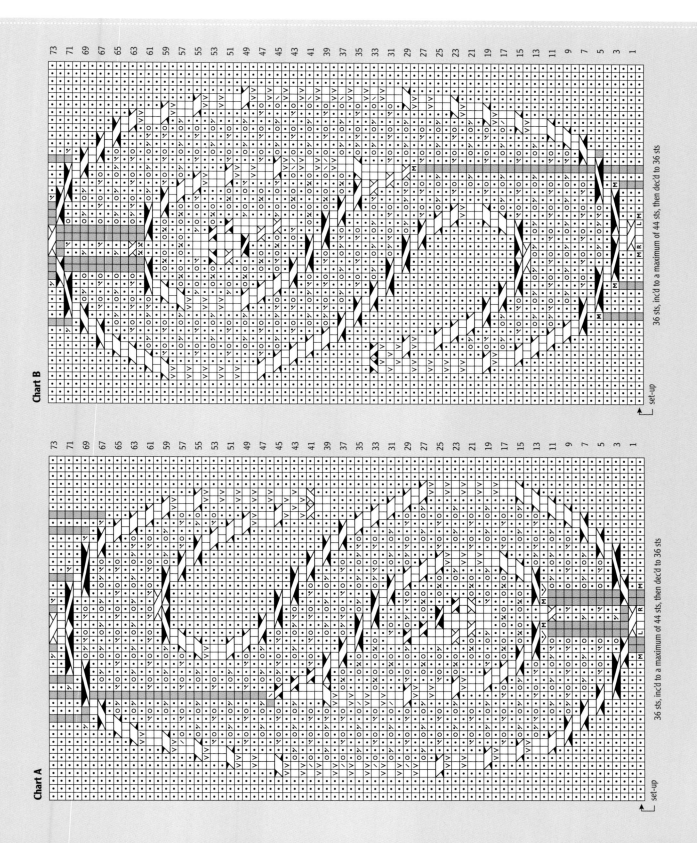

Chart B

73 71 69 67 65 63 61 59 57 55 53 51 49 47 45 43 41 39 37 35 33 31 29 27 25 23 21 19 17 15 13 11 9 7 5 3 1

36 sts, inc'd to a maximum of 44 sts, then dec'd to 36 sts

set-up

Chart A

73 71 69 67 65 63 61 59 57 55 53 51 49 47 45 43 41 39 37 35 33 31 29 27 25 23 21 19 17 15 13 11 9 7 5 3 1

36 sts, inc'd to a maximum of 44 sts, then dec'd to 36 sts

set-up

cloth and then the weaver paid the spinner for the yarn.

Woolens, worsteds, linen, and silk fabrics were sold in the small villages from the local weavers' cottages. In larger towns, the weavers represented their own goods or sold them to masters who transported them to established cloth markets known as "halls." These marketplaces were specialized as cotton, linen, or wool halls.

Spinning Cotton

Establishing a local cotton cloth industry was a problem. I don't mean to slight the otherwise thoroughly competent English handspinners, but the truth was they were confounded by the cotton fiber. They were adept at spinning flax, hemp, wool, and silk. (Silk production was an established industry in England because of the Silk Road centuries before.) Cotton was utterly different and very foreign. Spinners could produce a medium-fine yarn but were challenged when it

came to spinning gossamer thread for fashionably sheer fabrics. Typically, the handweaver would use linen yarn on the loom because local handspun cotton yarns would not hold up to the rigors of weaving. Handspun cotton yarn was instead put into the shuttle to pass back and forth across the linen warp. This wove up into a cotton-linen union cloth known as fustian.

Fustians were stiffer than 100 percent cotton fabrics because of the linen warp. This affected the drape and hand of the cloth. The linen yarn was also darker than cotton and did not take dye as well as imported 100 percent cotton fabrics.

Textiles and the Industrial Revolution

Jane Austen was born near the dawn of the Industrial Revolution. What we would recognize in the twentieth century as a factory system was just beginning to take form in a few cities.

The new factories housed all stages of manufacturing in one location.

Inventions came one after another. The spinning jenny permitted the handspinner to spin eight yarns at one time. The carding machine transformed lumpy raw fiber into an open, fluffy, easily spun form in a similar manner to the handcarder, only in greater amount and significantly faster. The fly shuttle took the shuttle from the weaver's hand, and the Arkwright water-powered frame spun yarn entirely by machine. These inventions were developed, improved, and ultimately adopted. In time, these machines were more productive than the handweaver and handspinner, but it didn't happen overnight.

Conversion from handspinning and handweaving to machine production took nearly one hundred years to spread throughout England, Scotland, and Ireland. There were rural pockets, however, where people continued to handspin yarns for their own use and for local specialties.

An 1860 engraving of a spinning jenny machine.

ISTOCKPHOTO.COM/DUNCAN WALKER (DUNCAN1890)

The Yarn in Jane Austen's Hands ∞ **105**

Knitting Yarn

It is a sure thing that there were no yarn stores as we know them today in Jane Austen's time. During the late eighteenth century, yarn for handknitting was most likely handspun (though in cities where cotton and wool mills proliferated, there would have been the opportunity for the occasional spindle of yarn to "fall off the truck"). New machine-spun yarn would have been tallied (or put into accounts) and in the pipeline for conversion to fabric. In other words, if the yarn were spun in the mill, it is unlikely that it would leave the mill in any form other than fabric.

Factories produced wool, silk, and cotton cloth. Ultimately, linen was machine spun, but it was after 1840 when the practice became widespread. For wool and linen, it is most likely that knitting yarns would have been handspun on a handspindle or a spinning wheel.

The Spindle

Yarn was spun in Great Britain on spindles originating in prehistoric times. The spindle is a simple tool—comprised of a stick (or shaft) and a weight (or whorl). As the spindle twirled like a top, it put twist into the wool or whatever fiber was used.

When the fiber was stretched as it was twisted (a process called drafting), it made yarn. After the spinner produced a length of yarn, she wound it onto the spindle and made another length. With her spindle, the spinner was free to walk and attend children or animals, her small work always in her pocket, always at hand. Spindle-spun yarn was dense and often firmly spun with a lot of twist.

The Wheel

So went the spinning of yarns, right up until the Middle Ages when influence from cotton- and silk-growing countries brought the yarns and the tools to make the yarns to England. The tool was a new kind of spindle, one that was laid on its side and held against a pair of short posts. A cord passed around the spindle and a large drive wheel, connecting them. When the wheel turned, so did the spindle, though much faster. This driven spindle could spin very fine, firmly twisted cotton and silk yarns. It could also spin good English wool and became known as the wool or muckle wheel.

There were a couple of wheel types in use in the time of Jane Austen. One, the familiar driven spindle wheel, produced a fuzzy, elastic woolen yarn from carded wool rolled into soft sausage-like shapes (rolags). The other was a more complex and subtle spinning device that both spun the yarn and wound it onto a bobbin. Yarns spun on this wheel were worsted, lean, and lustrous. The yarns were called "garnesey" or "jarsey" (jersey) yarns.

The spinning-room in Shadwell Rope Works.

Supply and Demand

Until the mid-nineteenth century when machines took over spinning, the output of the handspinner could not meet the needs of the weaver. It took five to seven spinners to supply a single weaver. (Weavers consume a prodigious volume of yarn.) On the other hand, it is said that a single handspinner could supply five knitters. That sounds better for both the spinner and the knitter, but consider the number of stockings, shawls, hats, scarves, and mittens that were needed in the community. How many knitting needles were constantly at work in even a small village that might have one or two looms? The handspinner never produced enough yarn.

Unless the spinner was infirm or aged, there were other chores that called for attention. She did not spend ten to twelve hours a day focused on spinning and then go home to a hot cooked meal like later factory workers. Spinning, child care, cooking, gardening, and brewing were integrated into seasonal patterns of a simple rural life.

Jane Austen's Yarn

To purchase her knitting yarn, Jane Austen could have made inquiries to find a local spinner or perhaps purchased a handspun skein while in London or at a shop like Fords, depicted in *Emma*. Wool or flax for Jane Austen's knitting yarn would have most likely come from local sources: sheep grazing on nearby fields or flax from a dooryard patch. The wool would have been washed and carded by hand, the flax handprocessed through the myriad steps to release the fiber from the plant stem and organize it into spinning form. All of this washing, carding, and flax-processing represents hours of handwork. It does not include time and attention attributed to the shepherd and gardener.

Yarn was spun in Great Britain on spindles originating in prehistoric times.

Compared to our current global yarn market, early-nineteenth-century yarn choices would have seemed meager indeed. This yarn most likely would have been white or a natural undyed color. If she wanted special color in her yarn, Jane Austen would have needed to contract with a dyer to do the job. The skeins she would be offered could have been of irregular length and could contain multiple knots. If the spinner had ready access to wool or flax or if Jane obtained the wool from her father's herd of Leicestershire sheep, then she would have had better choices.

Nevertheless, Jane would have paid good money for her handspun yarn because it represented use of resources. The material from which the yarn was made had intrinsic value. Time involved in its growing, processing, and production had worth. That meant that the textile knitted from the spinner's yarn would come to have its own value. Note that in her time, domestic textiles and clothing were considered prized possessions, to be listed and cataloged. What remains from that time are special-occasion clothing of well-to-do personages. Cloth and textiles were so dear that when the original item was repaired beyond use, it was remade into smaller and smaller items, until the scraps disintegrated to nothing.

From our vantage point, Jane's knitting yarn could certainly appear humble. She lived during the sunset hour for the handspinner. However, if perchance you would know yarn as Jane would, you might sidle up to a modern handspinner and ask to sample a yarn as Jane would have known it.

Dyepots litter the front yard; looms, books, and spinning wheels fill the house. Her daughter asks if maybe Mom "has an issue with too much fiber." No. It is just life as STEPHENIE GAUSTAD.

Resources

Braudel, Fernand. *The Perspective of the World, Civilization and Capitalism, 15th–18th Century,* New York: Harper and Row, 1984.

Horner, John. *The Linen Trade of Europe during the Spinning Wheel Period.* Belfast, Ireland: McCaw, Stevenson & Orr Ltd., 1920.

Kerridge, Eric. *Textile Manufactures in Early Modern England.* Manchester, United Kingdom: Manchester University Press, 1985.

Cottage Tea Cozy

JOANNA JOHNSON

Pastoral in setting and charming in scope, cottages are found throughout Jane Austen's novels: the Dashwood's Barton Cottage in *Sense and Sensibility,* Aunt Norris's cottage in *Mansfield Park,* and *Persuasion's* Uppercross Cottage come to mind. Nearly all of Jane Austen's novels were written from her home at Chawton Cottage, where she resided with her dear sister, Cassandra, and their mother. We can only imagine the conversations around the tea table in that place and how their society inspired Jane's beloved literary characters.

FINISHED SIZE About 22" (56 cm) circumference at base, 16" (40.5 cm) circumference at upper edge, and 9" (23 cm) tall including "roof" lid, after felting. To fit an average teapot.

YARN Bulky weight (#6 Super Bulky) *Shown here:* Brown Sheep Company Shepherd's Shades (100% wool; 131 yd [120 m]/3½ oz [100 g]): #SS416 lemon juice (MC), 1 skein; #SS542 marsh grass (CC, dark gold), 1 skein. Brown Sheep Company Waverly Woolcolors (100% wool; 8 yd [7.3 m]/⅕ oz [5.7 g]) mini-skein: 1 skein each of 9 colors: 7034w (dark gray), 1074w (light gray), 7131w (navy), 5013w (medium green), 5094w (light green), 2082w (violet), 2013w (rose), 3034w (peach), and 4081w (yellow).

NEEDLES Size 11 (8.0 mm): 16" (40.5 cm) circular (cir) and double-pointed (dpn). Adjust needle size if necessary to obtain the correct gauge.

NOTIONS Markers (m); stitch holders; tapestry needle; two ½" (1.3 cm) buttons.

GAUGE 11 sts and 20½ rows/rnds = 4" (10 cm) in St st, after felting.

Notes

- The body of the cozy (the cottage) is knit entirely with the main color; the door and windows are added using duplicate-stitch embroidery during finishing.

- This project uses Brown Sheep Company's Waverly Woolcolors for the embroidery. It is needlework wool available in 8-yard mini-skeins in over 400 colors. One skein is enough to embroider a pair of windows or the door as shown here, so have fun and add more of your own creative details if desired.

COTTAGE

Using cir needle and MC, CO 60 sts. Place marker (pm) and join for working in the rnd, being careful not to twist sts.

Rnd 1: K30, pm for side, k30.

Rnd 2: Purl.

Rnd 3: (inc rnd) K1, M1L, knit to 1 st before side m, M1R, k1, slip marker (sl m), k1, M1L, knit to last st, M1R, k1—4 sts inc'd.

Rnd 4: Knit.

Rnd 5: Rep Rnd 3—68 sts; 34 sts in each marked section.

Rnds 6 and 7: Knit.

Rnd 8: K34 to side m, remove m, then place next 34 sts on holder to be worked later for back of cottage—34 sts.

Front of Cottage

Work sts for front of cottage back and forth in rows as foll:

Row 1: (WS) Purl.

Row 2: (RS) Knit.

Row 3: Purl.

Row 4: (inc row) Knit 1, M1L, knit to last st, M1R, k1—2 sts inc'd.

Rows 5–8: Rep Rows 1–4 once more—38 sts.

Rows 9–17: Work 9 rows even in St st, beg and ending with a WS row.

Row 18: (dec row) K1, ssk, knit to last 3 sts, k2tog, k1—2 sts dec'd.

Row 19: Purl.

Row 20: Knit.

Row 21: Purl.

Row 22: Rep Row 18—34 sts.

Rows 23–25: Rep Rows 19–21.

Cut yarn and place sts on holder.

Return 34 held sts for back of cottage to cir needle. Rejoin yarn with RS facing and knit 1 RS row. Work Rows 1–25 as for front of cottage, ending with a WS row. Do not break yarn.

Joining row: (RS) Using yarn attached to back of cottage, k34, then k34 held sts for front of cottage—68 sts.

Work back and forth in rows as foll:

Row 1: (WS) Knit.

Row 2: (RS) K1, ★k2tog, k2; rep from ★ to last 3 sts, k2tog, k1—51 sts.

Rows 3–6: Knit 4 rows, ending with a RS row—3 garter ridges completed.

BO all sts kwise.

ROOF

Using cir needle and CC, CO 66 sts. Pm and join for working in the rnd, being careful not to twist sts. As you work the following instructions, change to dpn when there are too few sts to fit around the cir needle.

Rnd 1: Knit.

Rnd 2: Purl.

Rnds 3–6: Rep Rnds 1 and 2 twice—3 garter ridges completed.

Rnds 7–9: Knit.

Rnd 10: ★K9, k2tog; rep from ★—60 sts.

Rnds 11 and 12: Knit 2 rnds.

Rnd 13: ★K8, k2tog; rep from ★—54 sts.

Rnds 14 and 15: Knit 2 rnds.

Rnd 16: ★K7, k2tog; rep from ★—48 sts.

Rnds 17 and 18: Knit 2 rnds.

Rnd 19: ★K6, k2tog; rep from ★—42 sts.

Rnds 20 and 21: Knit 2 rnds.

Rnd 22: ★K5, k2tog; rep from ★—36 sts.

Rnd 23: Knit.

Rnd 24: ★K4, k2tog; rep from ★—30 sts.

Rnd 25: Knit.

Rnd 26: ★K3, k2tog; rep from ★—24 sts.

Rnd 27: Knit.

Rnd 28: *K2, k2tog; rep from *—18 sts.

Rnd 29: Knit.

Rnd 30: *K1, k2tog; rep from *—12 sts.

Rnd 31: K2tog 6 times—6 sts.

Rnds 32–34: Knit 3 rnds for "topknot" chimney.

Rnd 35: K2tog 3 times—3 sts.

Cut yarn, leaving an 8" (20 cm) tail. Thread tail through rem 3 sts, and fasten off on WS.

FINISHING

Door and Windows

Mark the center 20 sts on the front of the cottage to indicate the area for the Cottage embroidery diagram. Beg just above the purl rnd at the base of the cottage and using CC, work the cottage door in duplicate st according to the diagram. Using Waverly 7034w (dark gray), work the two windows in duplicate st according to the diagram.

Weave in all ends.

Felting

Felt the tea cozy cottage and roof using your favorite method; I used a top loading-washing machine on 15-minute cycle with hot water. The amount and speed of felting will vary depending on your machine and water conditions, so check the pieces frequently until they are the right size for your teapot. Shape pieces gently by hand, and allow to air-dry.

Embroidery

Use the photographs as a guide, or embroider the tea cozy according to your preferences. For a cozy as shown, work running st embroidery using 1074w (light gray) to outline the door and windows, and to create window lattices. Using 7131w (navy), make a French knot for doorknob. Using 5094w (light green), work straight sts for grass and flower stems. Using 5013w (medium green), use leaf sts to add leaves to stems. Using 2082w (violet), 2013w (rose), 3034w (peach), and 4081w (yellow), work French knot flowers.

Buttons and Button Loops

Using MC, make a 4-strand button loop centered on the 3 garter ridges at the top of the cozy as shown. Add a second button loop below the first, positioned to accommodate the handle of your teapot; for the cozy shown, the lower loop is about 3" (7.5 cm) below the first loop. Sew buttons to the other side of the opening, opposite the loops. ✽

JOANNA JOHNSON is the author and pattern designer of the knitting picture books *Phoebe's Sweater, Freddie's Blanket,* and *Phoebe's Birthday,* which are illustrated by her husband, Eric, and published by their independent press, Slate Falls Press (slatefallspress.com). She enjoys working with what she believes to be the perfect combination of materials: books and yarn.

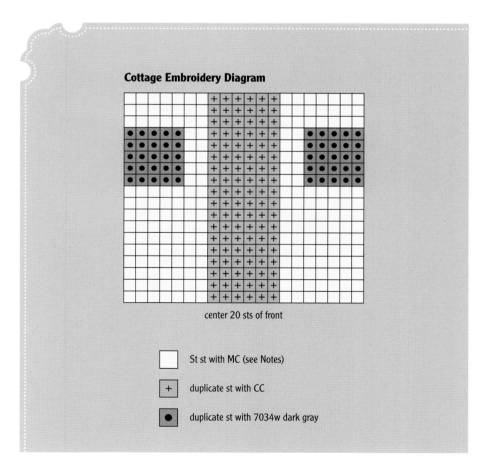

Cottage Embroidery Diagram

center 20 sts of front

☐ St st with MC (see Notes)

+ duplicate st with CC

● duplicate st with 7034w dark gray

Benwick Cardigan

KATHLEEN DAMES

This cardigan, trimmed with sharp braids and the requisite heart on its sleeve, will make you feel like the heroine in your own novel. The one-piece body and sleeves are worked separately to the underarms, then joined for working the saddle shoulder yoke. This cardigan features integrated braided front bands, saddle-shoulder shaping, cabled "epaulettes," and more braid at the collar, cuffs, and lower edge. Finishing is quick, with just the sleeves to seam and the underarms to graft. Hook-and-eyes complete the clean front finish associated with naval dress coats from the Regency era, such as one Captain Benwick of *Persuasion* might wear.

FINISHED SIZE 32 (34, 36, 38, 40, 42, 44)" (81.5 [86.5, 91.5, 96.5, 101.5, 106.5, 112] cm) bust circumference, closed. Cardigan shown measures 32" (81.5 cm).

YARN DK weight (#3 Light)
Shown here: String Theory Merino DK (100% superwash Merino; 280 yd [256 m]/4 oz [113 g]): cobalt, 4 (5, 5, 5, 5, 5, 5) skeins.

NEEDLES Size 6 (4 mm): two 29" (73.5 cm) or longer circular (cir). Adjust needle size if necessary to obtain the correct gauge, and choose a needle length close to desired chest circumference.

NOTIONS Markers (m); cable needle (cn); coil-less safety pins or locking stitch markers; stitch holders or waste yarn; tapestry needle; 7 hook-and-eye sets; sharp-point sewing needle and matching thread.

GAUGE 20 sts and 30 rows = 4" (10 cm) in St st; 8 sts of Vertical Aran Braid at each front edge measure about ¾" (2 cm) wide; 32 sts (8 patt reps) of Horizontal Aran Braid measure about 3¼" (8.5 cm) wide.

Notes

◆ *When working with the hand-dyed yarn shown, use the best-matching skeins for the sleeves, and blend the skeins in the body by switching between two skeins every two rows.*

◆ *The cardigan shown has a plain right sleeve and a heart on the left sleeve. If desired, you may choose to work both sleeves the same.*

2/2 RC: Sl 2 sts to cable needle (cn) and hold in back, k2, then k2 from cn.

2/2 LC: Sl 2 sts to cn and hold in front, k2, then k2 from cn.

K5TOG: Knit 5 sts together—4 sts dec'd. For an alternate method, sl 1 kwise, k3tog, pass slipped st over k3tog st on right needle, sl k3tog st to left needle, lift second st on left needle over k3tog st, then return k3tog st to right needle—4 sts dec'd.

HORIZONTAL ARAN BRAID
(multiple of 4 sts)
Row 1: (RS) *2/ 2 RC (see Stitch Guide); rep from * to end.

Row 2: Purl.

Row 3: K2, *2/ 2 LC (see Stitch Guide); rep from * to last 2 sts, k2.

Row 4: Purl.

Rep Rows 1–4 for patt.

VERTICAL ARAN BRAID
(worked over 8 sts)
Row 1: (RS) 2/ 2 RC twice.

Row 2: P8.

Row 3: K2, 2/ 2 LC, k2.

Row 4: P8.

Rep Rows 1–4 for patt.

RS BODY DEC ROW: Work in established patt to 1 st before first marked st at end of right front, k2tog (marked st tog with st before it); work to marked st at beg of back, ssk (marked st tog with st after it); knit to 1 st before marked st at end of back, k2tog (marked st tog with st before it); work to marked st at beg of left front, ssk (marked st tog with st after it); work in patt to end—4 sts dec'd: 1 st from each front and 2 back sts; no change to sleeve stitch counts.

WS BODY DEC ROW: Work in established patt to 1 st before first marked st at end of left front, ssp; work to marked st at beg of back, p2tog; purl to 1 st before marked st at end of back, ssp; work to marked st at beg of right front, p2tog; work in patt to end—4 sts dec'd: 1 st from each front and 2 back sts; no change to sleeve stitch counts.

RS SLEEVE DEC ROW: Work in established patt to first marked st at end of right front, ssk (marked st tog with sleeve st after it); work to 1 st before marked st at beg of back, k2tog (marked st tog with sleeve st before it); knit to marked st at end of back, ssk (marked st tog with sleeve st after it); work to 1 st before marked st at beg of left front, k2tog (marked st tog with sleeve st before it), work to end—4 sts dec'd: 2 sts from each sleeve; no change to body stitch counts.

WS SLEEVE DEC ROW: Work in established patt to marked st at end of left front, p2tog; work to 1 st before marked st at beg of back, ssp; purl to marked st at end of back, p2tog; work to 1 st before marked st at beg of right front, ssp, work to end—4 sts dec'd: 2 sts from each sleeve, no change to body st counts.

LOWER BODY

Using long-tail cast-on method, CO 320 (340, 360, 380, 400, 420, 440) sts. Purl 1 WS row. Work Rows 1–4 of Horizontal Aran Braid patt (see Stitch Guide) once, then work Rows 1–3 once more, ending with a RS row—8 rows total, including first purled row; piece measures about 1" (2.5 cm).

Dec row: (WS) P8, k2tog twice, [p2tog] 148 (158, 168, 178, 188, 198, 208) times to last 12 sts, k2tog twice, p8—168 (178, 188, 198, 208, 218, 228) sts.

Set-up row: (RS) Work Row 1 of Vertical Aran Braid (see Stitch Guide) over 8 sts, p2, knit to last 10 sts, p2, work Row 1 of Vertical Aran Braid over 8 sts.

Working braid patts as established at each front edge, work 2 sts next to each braid in rev St st (purl on RS, knit on WS), and work rem sts in between in St st until piece measures 14 (14½, 14½, 14¾, 14¾, 15, 15)" (35.5 [37, 37, 37.5, 37.5, 38, 38] cm) from CO, ending with a RS row.

Dividing row: (WS) Work 8 braid sts as established, k2, p30 (32, 34, 36, 38, 40, 42) left front sts, purl the next 12 (14, 14, 16, 16, 18, 18) sts and place these just-worked sts on stitch holder or waste yarn for left underarm, p64 (66, 72, 74, 80, 82, 88) back sts, purl the next 12 (14, 14, 16, 16, 18, 18) sts and place these just-worked sts on stitch holder or waste yarn for right underarm, p30 (32, 34, 36, 38, 40, 42) right front sts, k2, work 8 braid sts as established—144 (150, 160, 166, 176, 182, 192) sts rem on needle; 40 (42, 44, 46, 48, 50, 52) sts each front, and 64 (66, 72, 74, 80, 82, 88) back sts.

Make a note of the braid row just completed so you can resume the pattern in the yoke later with the correct row. Set aside.

PLAIN SLEEVE

Using empty cir needle and long-tail cast-on method, CO 80 (80, 88, 88, 88, 96, 96) sts. Purl 1 WS row. Work Rows 1–4 of Horizontal Aran Braid patt once, then work Rows 1–3 once more, ending with a RS row—8 rows total, including first purled row; piece measures about 1" (2.5 cm).

Dec row: (WS) [P2tog] 40 (40, 44, 44, 44, 48, 48) times—40 (40, 44, 44, 44, 48, 48) sts rem.

Work 4 rows even in St st, ending with a WS row.

Inc row: (RS) K1, M1L, knit to last st, M1R, k1—2 sts inc'd.

Cont in St st, [work 5 rows even, then rep the inc row] 10 (12, 11, 12, 15, 14, 15) times, working new sts in St st— 62 (66, 68, 70, 76, 78, 80) sts. Work even in St st until piece measures 17 (17½, 17¾, 18, 18¼, 18¼, 18¼)" (43 [44.5, 45, 45.5, 46.6, 46.5, 46.5] cm) from CO, or desired length to underarm, ending with a WS row. Place the first 6 (7, 7, 8, 8, 9, 9) sts and last 6 (7, 7, 8, 8, 9, 9) sts on separate waste yarn or holders for underarm, then place 50 (52, 54, 54, 60, 60, 62) center sts on another holder. Break yarn and set aside.

HEART SLEEVE

Work as for plain sleeve until all incs have been completed—62 (66, 68, 70, 76, 78, 80) sts. Work even in St st until sleeve measures 13 (13½, 13¾, 14, 14¼, 14¼, 14¼)" (33 [34.5, 35, 35.5, 36, 36, 36] cm) from CO edge ending with a WS row. Work 4 rows even in rev St st.

Set-up row: (RS) P23 (25, 26, 27, 30, 31, 32), place marker (pm), work Row 1 of Embossed Heart chart over 15 sts (inc them to 17 sts as shown), pm, p24 (26, 27, 28, 31, 32, 33).

Keeping sts on each side of chart section in rev St st, work Rows 2–13 of chart, inc chart section to a maximum of 21 sts, then dec back to 15 sts as shown—62 (66, 68, 70, 76, 78, 80) sts again. Work 4 rows even in rev St st.

Change to working all sts in St st, and work even until sleeve measures 17 (17½, 17¾, 18, 18¼, 18¼, 18¼)" (43 [44.5, 45, 45.5, 46.6, 46.5, 46.5] cm) from CO, ending with a WS row. Place first 6 (7, 7, 8, 8, 9, 9) and last 6 (7, 7, 8, 8, 9, 9) sts on separate waste yarn or holders for underarms, then place 50 (52, 54, 54, 60, 60, 62) center sts on another holder. Break yarn and set aside.

YOKE

Note: Removable markers are placed directly in the stitches themselves, and not on the needle between stitches; move these markers up as you work so you can continue to identify each marked stitch throughout the yoke.

Joining row: (RS) Using empty cir needle, work 8 braid sts as established, p2, k30 (32, 34, 36, 38, 40, 42) right front sts, then place a removable m in the last st of right front; return 50 (52, 54, 54, 60, 60, 62) held sts of plain sleeve to needle and knit across them; knit across 64 (66, 72, 74, 80, 82, 88) sts for back, placing removable m in the first and last back sts; return 50 (52, 54, 54, 60, 60, 62) held sts of heart sleeve to needle and knit across them; placing a removable

m in the first front st, k30 (32, 34, 36, 38, 40, 42) left front sts, p2, work 8 braid sts as established—244 (254, 268, 274, 296, 302, 316) sts; 40 (42, 44, 46, 48, 50, 52) sts each front, 50 (52, 54, 54, 60, 60, 62) sts each sleeve, 64 (66, 72, 74, 80, 82, 88) back sts.

Next row: (WS) Work 8 braid sts as established, k2, purl to last 10 sts, k2, work 8 braid sts as established.

Set up epaulette braids: (RS) Work in established patt to first marked st at end of right front, knit marked st; ★work sleeve sts as k21 (22, 23, 23, 26, 26, 27), p2, [sl 1 st to cn and hold in back, work k1f&b, then work k1f&b in st from cn] 2 times, p2, k21 (22, 23, 23, 26, 26, 27)★; knit to marked st at end of back, knit marked st, rep from ★ to ★ for second sleeve, work in established patt to end of row—4 sts inc'd each sleeve;

Embossed Heart Chart

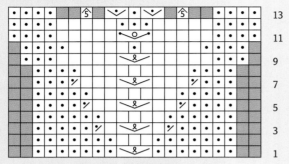

15 sts inc'd to 21 sts, then dec'd to 15 sts

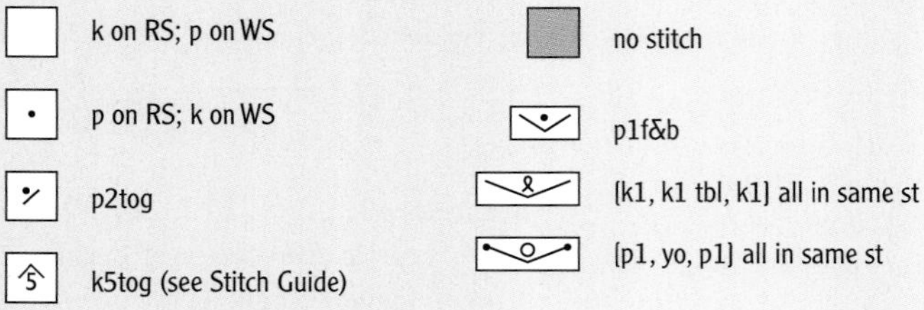

□	k on RS; p on WS	
·	p on RS; k on WS	
⟋	p2tog	
Ŝ	k5tog (see Stitch Guide)	

▨	no stitch
⌄	p1f&b
⟑	[k1, k1 tbl, k1] all in same st
⌣	[p1, yo, p1] all in same st

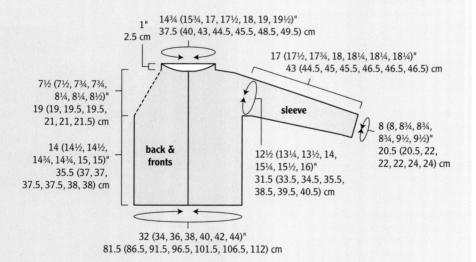

1"
2.5 cm

14¾ (15¾, 17, 17½, 18, 19, 19½)"
37.5 (40, 43, 44.5, 45.5, 48.5, 49.5) cm

17 (17½, 17¾, 18, 18¼, 18¼, 18¼)"
43 (44.5, 45, 45.5, 46.5, 46.5, 46.5) cm

7½ (7½, 7¾, 7¾,
8¼, 8¼, 8½)"
19 (19, 19.5, 19.5,
21, 21, 21.5) cm

sleeve

14 (14½, 14½,
14¾, 14¾, 15, 15)"
35.5 (37, 37,
37.5, 37.5, 38, 38) cm

back &
fronts

8 (8, 8¾, 8¾,
8¾, 9½, 9½)"
20.5 (20.5, 22,
22, 22, 24, 24) cm

12½ (13¼, 13½, 14,
15¼, 15½, 16)"
31.5 (33.5, 34.5, 35.5,
38.5, 39.5, 40.5) cm

32 (34, 36, 38, 40, 42, 44)"
81.5 (86.5, 91.5, 96.5, 101.5, 106.5, 112) cm

---

54 (56, 58, 58, 64, 64, 66) sts each sleeve, no change to front and back stitch counts.

Next row: (WS) ★Work in established patt to sleeve, work sleeve sts as p21 (22, 23, 23, 26, 26, 27), k2, p8, k2, p21 (22, 23, 23, 26, 26, 27); rep from ★ once more, work in established patt to end of row.

Next row: (RS) ★Work in established patt to center 12 sleeve sts, p2, work Row 1 of Vertical Aran Braid over 8 sts, p2; rep from ★ once more, work in established patt to end of row.

Note: If the epaulette and front braid patterns do not happen to be on the same row, keep track of them separately.

Working braid patts as established with 2 sts on each side of both epaulette braids in rev St st, work in established patt until yoke measures 1 (1¼, 1, 1, 1, 1¼, 1)" (2.5 [3.2, 2.5, 2.5, 2.5, 3.2, 2.5] cm) from joining row.

SHAPE ARMHOLES
Work body dec rows (see Stitch Guide) according to your size as foll:

SIZES 32 (36, 38)"
Work RS Body Dec row, then work 1 WS row even—248 (272, 278) sts: 39 (43, 45) sts each front, 54 (58, 58) sts each sleeve, 62 (70, 72) back sts.

SIZE 34"
Omit this shaping and skip to *For all sizes* below—no change to stitch counts.

SIZE 40"
Work RS body dec row, WS body dec row, RS body dec row, then work 1 WS row even—292 sts; 45 sts each front, 64 sts each sleeve, 74 back sts.

SIZE 42"
Work RS body dec row, then WS body dec row—302 sts; 48 sts each front, 64 sts each sleeve, 78 back sts.

SIZE 44"
[Work RS body dec row, work WS body dec row] 2 times—308 sts; 48 sts each front, 66 sts each sleeve, 80 back sts.

FOR ALL SIZES
Yoke measures 1¼ (1¼, 1¼, 1¼, 1½, 1½, 1½)" (3.2 [3.2, 3.2, 3.2, 3.8, 3.8, 3.8] cm) from joining row.

Shape Sleeve Caps
SIZES 32 (36, 38, 44)"
[Work RS sleeve dec row, work WS sleeve dec row] 10 (11, 11, 13) times, work RS sleeve dec row, then work 1 WS row even—164 (180, 186, 200) sts; 39 (43, 45, 48) sts each front, 12 sts each sleeve for all sizes, 62 (70, 72, 80) back sts.

SIZES (34, 40, 42)"
[Work RS sleeve dec row, work WS sleeve dec row] (11, 13, 13) times— (174, 188, 198) sts; (42, 45, 48) sts each front, 12 sts each sleeve for all sizes, (66, 74, 78) back sts.

FOR ALL SIZES
Yoke measures 4¼ (4¼, 4½, 4½, 5, 5, 5¼)" (11 [11, 11.5, 11.5, 12.5, 12.5, 13.5] cm) from joining row.

[Work RS body dec row, work WS body dec row] 5 times for all sizes—124 (134, 140, 146, 148, 158, 160) sts; 29 (32, 33, 35, 35, 38, 38) sts each front, 12 sts each sleeve, 42 (46, 50, 52, 54, 58, 60) back sts; yoke measures 5½ (5½, 5¾, 5¾, 6¼, 6¼, 6½)" (14 [14, 14.5, 14.5, 16, 16, 16.5] cm) from joining row.

Work short-rows across right saddle sts as foll:

Short-row 1: (RS) Work in established patt across right front and right sleeve to marked st at beg of back, ssk (marked st tog with st after it), turn—1 back st dec'd.

Short row 2: (WS) Sl 1 st pwise wyf, work in established patt to marked st at beg of right front sts, p2tog (marked st tog with st after it), turn—1 right front st dec'd.

Short-row 3: Sl 1 st kwise wyb, work in established patt to marked st at beg of back, ssk (marked st tog with st after it), turn—1 back st dec'd.

Rep Short-rows 2 and 3 (do not rep Short-row 1) 5 (6, 6, 7, 7, 8, 8) more times, but do not turn at the end of

the last RS Short-row 3—23 (25, 26, 27, 27, 29, 29) right front sts, 12 right sleeve sts, 35 (38, 42, 43, 45, 48, 50) back sts; no change to other stitch counts. With RS still facing, work in patt to end across rem back sts, left sleeve, and left front.

Work short-rows across left saddle sts as foll:

Short-row 1: (WS) Work in established patt across left front and left sleeve to marked st at beg of back, p2tog (marked st tog with st after it), turn—1 back st dec'd.

Short row 2: (RS) Sl 1 st kwise wyb, work in established patt to marked st at beg of left front sts, ssk (marked st tog with st after it), turn—1 left front st dec'd.

Short-row 3: Sl 1 st pwise wyf, work in established patt to marked st at beg of back, p2tog (marked st tog with st after it), turn—1 back st dec'd.

Rep Short-rows 2 and 3 (do not rep Short-row 1) 5 (6, 6, 7, 7, 8, 8) more times, but do not turn at the end of the last WS Short-row 3—98 (104, 110, 112, 114, 120, 122) sts; 23 (25, 26, 27, 27, 29, 29) sts each front, 12 sts each sleeve, 28 (30, 34, 34, 36, 38, 40) back sts; no significant change to yoke height at center front and back.

Work short-rows across back sts as foll:

Short-row 1: (WS) Work across back sts to marked st at end of back, p2tog (last back st tog with sleeve st after it), turn—1 right sleeve st dec'd.

Short-row 2: (RS) Work across back sts to marked st at end of back, ssk (last back st tog with sleeve st after it), turn—1 left sleeve st dec'd.

Rep Short-rows 1 and 2 for back 5 more times for all sizes—86 (92, 98, 100, 102, 108, 110) sts; 23 (25, 26, 27, 27, 29, 29) sts each front, 6 sts each sleeve, 28 (30, 34, 34, 36, 38, 40) back sts. With RS still facing, work to end across left sleeve and left front.

Next row: (WS) Work even in patt.

Next row: (RS) *Work in patt to 6 sleeve sts, k2tog 3 times; rep from * once more, work in patt to end—80 (86, 92, 94, 96, 102, 104) sts; 3 sts each sleeve, no change to front and back stitch counts; yoke measures about 7½ (7½, 7¾, 7¾, 8¼, 8¼, 8½)" (19 [19, 19.5, 19.5, 21, 21, 21.5] cm) at center back, and about 2" (5 cm) less at center front.

COLLAR
Inc row: (WS) Work 8 braid sts as established, p1f&b 64 (70, 76, 78, 80, 86, 88) times, work 8 sts braid sts as established—144 (156, 168, 172, 176, 188, 192) sts.

Work Rows 1–4 of Horizontal Aran Braid patt once, then work Rows 1–3 once more, ending with a RS row— collar measures about 1" (2.5 cm) high.

Work BO on next WS row as foll:

K2tog, *p2tog (2 sts on right needle), BO 1 st, k2tog (2 sts on right needle), BO 1 st; rep from * until 1 st rem, then fasten off last st.

FINISHING
Weave in ends. Block pieces to measurements. With yarn threaded on a tapestry needle, sew sleeve seams, then graft held underarm sts together using Kitchener st (see Glossary). With sewing thread and needle, sew hook-and-eye sets to WS of fronts so the edges of the front braids meet when the garment is closed. Position the highest set at the base of the collar, the lowest set 1½" (3.8 cm) up from CO edge, and the rem 5 sets evenly spaced in between. ♣

KATHLEEN DAMES designs and knits in New York City and Bath, Maine, with her very own Captain Wentworth and their three children. All of Jane Austen's works have provided her with joy and inspiration. You can find more of Kathleen's designs at kathleendames.blogspot .com, and she goes by the username Purly on Ravelry.

Marianne Dashwood Stockings

ANN KINGSTONE

In Regency England, ladies' stockings were invariably worn with a garter, a knitted or silk ribbon tied either just above or just below the knee to hold the stockings up. While most stockings were plain, many had "clocks," embroidered or integral lace decorations on the inner and outer legs. These two elements of Regency stockings, garters and clocks, feature prominently in these stockings inspired by Marianne Dashwood of *Sense and Sensibility*. A picot hem creates the casing for a pretty ribbon garter, while the lace clocks elegantly grace the legs.

FINISHED SIZE 6¾ (7½, 8½)" (17 [19, 21.5] cm) foot circumference, 9¾ (11¼, 12½)" (25 [28.5, 31.5] cm) calf circumference, and 8¼ (8¾, 9¼)" (21 [22, 23.5] cm) long from back of heel to tip of toe (see Notes). Stockings shown measure 7½" (19 cm).

YARN Lace weight (#0 Lace)
Shown here: Natural Dye Studio Dazzling (55% British Bluefaced Leicester, 45% silk; 437 yd [400 m]/100 g): lilac C17, 2 skeins.

NEEDLES Sizes 0 and 1 (2 and 2.25 mm). (See Notes.) Adjust needle sizes if necessary to obtain the correct gauge.

NOTIONS Markers (m); stitch holder or waste yarn; 1 yd (1 m) of waste yarn for provisional CO; tapestry needle; 1¾ yd (1.5 m) of ¼" (6 mm) ribbon.

GAUGE 35 sts and 48 rnds = 4" (10 cm) in St st on larger needles.

Notes

❖ These stockings are intended to be worn with about 10% negative ease.

❖ These socks can be worked using a set of 4 or 5 double-pointed needles, 2 circular needles, 1 long circular needle for the Magic Loop method, or 1 short circular needle.

❖ In keeping with the traditional stocking-knitting styles of Regency England, the socks include a false seam at the back of the leg, created by purling the center back stitch in every round.

❖ During the gusset setup, a neat finish is obtained by knitting into the back of each stitch picked up from the edges of the heel flap.

"Two delightful twilight walks...where the trees were the oldest and the grass was the longest and wettest, had—assisted by the still greater imprudence of sitting in her wet shoes and stockings—given Marianne a cold so violent, as, though for a day or two trifled with or denied, would force itself by increasing ailments, on the concern of everybody, and the notice of herself."

— Sense and Sensibility

STOCKINGS

Cuff

With smaller needles and using a provisional method (see Glossary), CO 84 (98, 112) sts. Place marker (pm) and join in the rnd. Knit 10 rnds.

Picot rnd: ★Yo, k2tog; rep from ★ around. Change to larger needles. Knit 6 rnds.

Eyelet rnd: ★Yo, k2tog, k5; rep from ★ around. Knit 3 rnds. Remove provisional CO and place sts onto smaller needles. Fold cuff at picot rnd with WS tog.

Joining rnd: Holding provisional sts behind working needles, ★k2tog (1 st from front needle and 1 st from back needle); rep from ★ around—84 (98, 112) sts.

Leg

SIZE 6¾" ONLY

Next rnd: P1, M1, k42, M1, knit to end—86 sts.

SIZE 7½" ONLY

Next rnd: P1, knit to end.

SIZE 8½" ONLY

Next rnd: P1, k2tog, k54, k2tog, knit to end—110 sts rem.

ALL SIZES

Next rnd: P1, knit to end. Cont in patt until piece measures 4½" (11.5 cm) from top of cuff.

Lace Clocks

Set-up rnd: P1, k14 (17, 20), pm, k15, pm, k27 (33, 39), pm, k15, pm for new beg-of-rnd (leave old beg-of-rnd m in place).

Next rnd: Knit to m, p1, knit to m, work Row 1 of Lace Clock chart over 15 sts, sl m, knit to m, work Row 1 of Lace Clock chart over 15 sts. Cont in patt through Row 15 of chart. Shape leg as

Lace Clock Chart

Fagoting Chart

			o	\	
/	o				1

- ☐ k on RS; p on WS
- o yo
- / k2tog
- \ ssk on RS; ssp on WS
- ⋀ sl 2 as if to k2tog, k1, p2sso

foll and, *at the same time,* work Rows 16–20 of chart once, then rep Rows 21–24 as needed.

Dec rnd: Knit to 2 sts before m, ssk, p1, k2tog, knit to m, work lace patt to m, k2tog, knit to 2 sts before m, ssk, work lace patt to m—4 sts dec'd. Rep dec rnd every 8th rnd 6 (7, 8) more times—58 (66, 74) sts rem. Work even in patt until piece measures about 14" (35.5 cm) from top of cuff, or desired length to heel, ending with Row 24 of chart.

Heel Flap

Set-up row: K7 (9, 11), p1, k7 (9, 11), sl m, work Row 1 of Fagoting chart, pm, k3, then place next 29 (33, 37) sts onto holder or waste yarn for instep—29 (33, 37) sts rem for heel flap. Work back and forth on these sts as foll:

Row 1: (WS) Sl 1 pwise wyf, p2, work Row 2 of Fagoting chart, p7 (9, 11), k1, p7 (9, 11), work Row 2 of Fagoting chart, pm, p3.

Row 2: (RS) Sl 1 kwise wyb, k2, work Row 1 of chart, k7 (9, 11), p1, k7 (9, 11), work Row 1 of chart, k3.

Rep last 2 rows 11 (13, 15) more times, then work Row 1 once more.

Heel Turn

Note: Remove m as you come to them.

Set-up row 1: (RS) Sl 1 kwise wyb, k16 (18, 20), ssk, k1, turn.

Set-up row 2: (WS) Sl 1 pwise wyf, p6, p2tog, p1, turn.

Row 1: (RS) Sl 1 kwise wyb, knit to 1 st before gap, ssk, k1, turn.

Row 2: (WS) Sl 1 pwise wyf, purl to 1 st before gap, p2tog, p1, turn.

Rep Rows 1 and 2 three (4, 5) more times—19 (21, 23) heel sts rem.

Next row: (RS) Sl 1 kwise wyb, knit to 1 st before gap, ssk, turn.

Next row: (WS) Sl 1 pwise wyf, purl to 1 st before gap, p2tog, turn—17 (19, 21) heel sts rem.

Gusset

Set-up row: (RS) Sl 1 pwise wyb, k16 (18, 20) heel sts, pick up and knit 12 (14, 16) sts along side of heel flap, work held instep sts as foll: K4, pm, work Row 2 of Fagoting chart, k13 (17, 21), work Row 1 of Fagoting chart, pm, k4; pick up and knit 12 (14, 16) sts along side of heel flap, k17 (19, 21) heel sts, k12 (14, 16) gusset sts (see Notes), pm for new beg of rnd—70 (80, 90) sts total.

Dec rnd 1: Work in patt to last 3 sts, k2tog, k1—1 st dec'd.

Dec rnd 2: Work 29 (33, 37) sts in patt, k1, ssk, knit to end—1 st dec'd.

Rep last 2 rnds 5 (6, 7) more times—58 (66, 74) sts rem.

Foot

Work even in patt until piece measures 1½" (3.8 cm) from end of gusset. Change to St st.

Next rnd: Remove all m except beg-of-rnd m and pm as foll: K29 (33, 37), pm, knit to end. Work even until piece measures 6¼ (6¾, 7¼)" (16 [17, 18.5] cm) from back of heel, or 2" (5 cm) less than desired finished length.

Toe

Dec rnd: K1, ssk, knit to 3 sts before m, k2tog, k2, ssk, knit to the last 3 sts, k2tog, k1—4 sts dec'd.

Next rnd: Knit. Rep last 2 rnds 6 (7, 8) more times—30 (34, 38) sts rem. Work dec rnd only 3 (4, 5) times—18 sts rem.

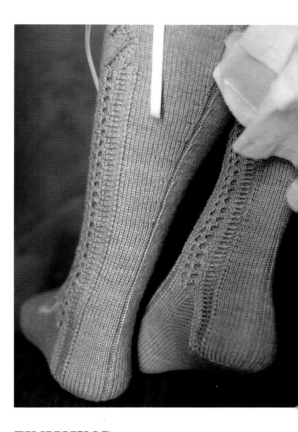

FINISHING

Break yarn, leaving a 12" (30.5 cm) tail. Graft toe using Kitchener st (see Glossary). Weave in loose ends. Block by soaking socks in lukewarm water until they are thoroughly wet, then gently pressing out excess water. Stretch damp socks on sock blockers or pin out to shape until dry. Cut ribbon in half. Thread each piece through eyelets at top of sock. ❧

ANN KINGSTONE is a British designer living in the beautiful county of Yorkshire, her lifelong home. Her designs include many that were inspired by works of British literature, beautifully presented in *Novel Knits,* Ann's first book. More details of this and Ann's full pattern range may be found at her website, annkingstone.com.

Elegant Gloves

HEATHER ZOPPETTI

Long gloves were a fashion staple during the Regency era. They reached above the elbow but often slipped down and pooled around the wrist. Sometimes the tops were held up with garters or ribbons. These elegant gloves start at the top with delicate scallops. A lace pattern creates a long-stemmed flower down the length of the arm and terminates on the back of the hand. A pretty ribbon threaded through garter-stitch eyelets helps hold them up.

FINISHED SIZE 10¼ (10¾, 12)" (26 [27.5, 30.5] cm) upper arm circumference, 7¼ (8, 8¼)" (18.5 [20.5, 21] cm) hand circumference, and 13½ (14¼, 14½)" (34.5 [36, 37] cm) long from CO edge to wrist. Gloves shown measure 10¾" (27.5 cm) at upper arm and 14¼" (36 cm) long.

YARN Fingering weight (#1 Super Fine) *Shown here:* Schachenmayr Regia Silk 4-ply (55% Merino, 25% nylon, 20% silk; 218 yd [199 m]/1¾ oz [50 g]): #001, white, 3 skeins for all sizes. Yarn distributed by Westminster Fibers.

NEEDLES Size 3 (3.25 mm): set of 4 or 5 double-pointed needles (dpn). Adjust needle size if necessary to obtain the correct gauge.

NOTIONS Markers (m); stitch holders; tapestry needle; 2½ yd (2.5 m) ribbon ¼" (6 mm) wide.

GAUGE 28 sts and 44 rnds = 4" (10 cm) in St st and chart patts.

Diamond Chart

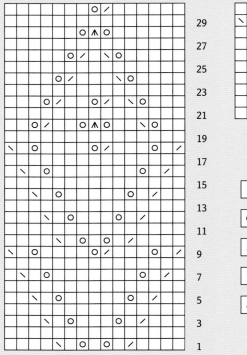

15 sts

Chevron Chart

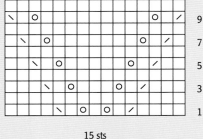

15 sts

	knit
O	yo
/	k2tog
\	ssk
∧	sl 2 as if to k2tog, k1, p2sso

ARM

Note: *The upper arm is worked the same for both the right and left gloves.*

CO 90 (95, 105) sts, but do not join in the rnd.

Set-up row: (RS) *Yo, k5, then one at a time pass fourth, third, second, and first sts of the k5 over the fifth st of the k5; rep from * to end—36 (38, 42) sts rem.

With RS still facing, place marker (pm) and join for working in the rnd, being careful not to twist sts.

Work lace border as foll:

Rnd 1: *Work [k1, yo, k1tbl] all in yo of set-up rnd, k1; rep from * to end—72 (76, 84) sts.

Rnd 2: *K1, k1tbl, k2; rep from * to end.

Rnds 3–5: Purl 1 rnd, knit 1 rnd, purl 1 rnd.

Rnd 6 (eyelet rnd): *Yo, k2tog; rep from * to end.

Rnds 7–9: Rep Rnds 3–5 once more—piece measures about 1" (2.5 cm) from deepest curve of scalloped edge.

Next rnd: K29 (31, 35), pm, work Rnd 1 of Chevron chart over 15 sts, pm, k28 (30, 34).

Working sts on each side of the marked chart section in St st, work Rnds 2–10 of chart.

Dec rnd: K1, k2tog, knit to m, slip marker (sl m), work 15 sts in established chart patt, sl m, knit to last 2 sts, ssk—2 sts dec'd.

Cont in established patts, [work 11 (13, 11) rnds even, then rep the dec rnd] 9 (7, 3) times—52 (60, 76) sts rem. Cont in established patts, [work 9 (11, 9) rnds even, then rep the dec rnd] 2 (3, 10) times, ending with Rnd 9 (5,

7) of chart—48 (54, 56) sts rem; 139 (145, 147) chart rnds completed; piece measures 13½ (14¼, 14½)" (34.5 [36, 37] cm) from CO.

Place sts on a holder to work later for right hand. Make a second arm in the same manner, but leave sts on dpn.

LEFT HAND

Notes: *As you work the following instructions, work 1 (5, 3) more rnd(s) of the Chevron chart to end with Rnd 10, then change to working the 15 marked sts according to the Diamond chart for the back of the hand. When Rnd 30 of the Diamond chart has been completed, remove the markers on each side of the chart section and work the stitches in stockinette.*

Thumb Gusset

K12 (14, 14), pm for gusset, k1, pm for gusset, work in patt to end—1 gusset st between m; rnd begins in center of palm.

Inc rnd: Work in patt to gusset m, sl m, M1, knit to next gusset m, M1, sl m, work in patt to end—2 sts inc'd between gusset m.

Cont in established patts, [work 3 rnds even, then rep the inc rnd] 7 (8, 8) times—17 (19, 19) gusset sts between m. Cont in established patts [work 1 rnd even, then rep the inc rnd] 0 (0, 1) time(s)—64 (72, 76) sts total; 17 (19, 21) gusset sts between m.

Next rnd: Work in patt to gusset m, place 17 (19, 21) thumb sts on holder, use the backward-loop method to CO 3 sts across thumb gap, work in patt to end—50 (56, 58) sts.

Work even in patt until piece measures 1" (2.5 cm) above the thumb gap and about 3¾ (4¼, 4½)" (9.5 [11, 11.5] cm) from base of thumb gusset. Remove beg-of-rnd m, work 38 (43, 44) sts in patt, replace m for new beg of rnd at little-finger side of hand.

Little Finger
K5 (6, 6), place next 40 (44, 46) sts on holder, use the backward-loop method to CO 1 st, k5 (6, 6)—11 (13, 13) sts. Work even in St st until little finger measures about 2¼" (5.5 cm) or just below the tip of wearer's finger.

Dec rnd: K2tog 4 (5, 5) times, k3tog—5 (6, 6) sts rem. Cut yarn leaving a 5" (12.5 cm) tail. Draw tail through rem sts, pull tight to close hole, and fasten off on WS.

Upper Hand
Return 40 (44, 46) held sts to needles, and rejoin yarn to beg of sts with RS facing. Knit to end, pick up and knit 2 sts from st CO at base of little finger, pm, and join for working in the rnd—42 (46, 48) sts. Work even in St st for ¼" (6 mm)—hand measures about 4 (4½, 4¾)" (10 [11.5, 12] cm) from base of thumb gusset.

Ring Finger
K7 (8, 8), place next 28 (30, 32) sts on holder, use the backward-loop method to CO 2 sts, k7 (8, 8), pm, and join for working in the rnd—16 (18, 18) sts. Work even in St st until ring finger measures about 2¾" (7 cm) or just below the tip of wearer's finger.

Dec rnd: K2tog 8 (9, 9) times—8 (9, 9) sts rem. Cut yarn leaving a 5" (12.5 cm) tail, and close tip as for little finger.

Middle Finger
Return 28 (30, 32) held sts to needles, and rejoin yarn to beg of sts with RS facing. K7 (7, 8), place next 14 (16, 16) sts on holder, use the backward-loop method to CO 2 sts, k7 (7, 8), pick up

and knit 2 sts from sts CO at base of ring finger, pm, and join for working in the rnd—18 (18, 20) sts. Work even in St st until middle finger measures about 3" (7.5 cm) or just below the tip of wearer's finger.

Dec rnd: K2tog 9 (9, 10) times—9 (9, 10) sts rem. Cut yarn leaving a 5" (12.5 cm) tail, and close tip as for little finger.

Index Finger
Return 14 (16, 16) held sts to needles, and rejoin yarn to beg of sts with RS facing. K14 (16, 16), then pick up and knit 2 sts from sts CO at base of middle finger, pm, and join for working in the rnd—16 (18, 18) sts. Work even in St st until index finger measures about 2¾" (7 cm) or just below the tip of wearer's finger.

Dec rnd: K2tog 8 (9, 9) times—8 (9, 9) sts rem. Cut yarn leaving 5" (12.5 cm) tail, and close tip as for little finger.

Thumb
Return 17 (19, 21) held thumb gusset sts to needles, and rejoin yarn to beg of sts with RS facing. K17 (19, 21), then pick up and knit 4 sts from 3 sts CO across thumb gap—21 (23, 25) sts.

Next rnd: K2tog, knit to last 6 sts, ssk, k4—19 (21, 23) sts. Work even in St st until thumb measures about 2" (5 cm) or just below the tip of wearer's thumb.

Dec rnd: K2tog 8 (9, 10) times, k3tog—9 (10, 11) sts rem. Cut yarn leaving 5" (12.5 cm) tail, and close tip as for little finger.

RIGHT HAND
Note: As for the left hand, work 1 (5, 3) more rnd(s) of the Chevron chart to end with Rnd 10, change to working the 15 marked sts according to the Diamond chart for the back of

the hand until Rnd 30 of the Diamond chart has been completed, and then remove the markers on each side of the chart section and work the stitches in St st.

Return 48 (54, 56) held arm sts to needles, and rejoin yarn to beg of sts with RS facing. K36 (40, 42), pm for gusset, k1, pm for gusset, knit to end of rnd—1 gusset st between m; rnd begins in center of palm. Work as for left-hand thumb gusset until all gusset incs have been completed—64 (72, 76) sts total; 17 (19, 21) gusset sts between m.

Next rnd: Work in patt to gusset m, place 17 (19, 21) thumb sts on holder, use the backward-loop method to CO 3 sts across thumb gap, work in patt to end—50 (56, 58) sts.

Work even in patt until piece measures 1" (2.5 cm) above the thumb gap and about 3¾ (4¼, 4½)" (9.5 [11, 11.5] cm) from base of thumb gusset. Remove beg-of-rnd m, work 12 (14, 14) sts in patt, replace m for new beg of rnd at little-finger side of hand.

Complete little finger, upper hand, ring finger, middle finger, index finger, and thumb as for left hand.

FINISHING
Weave in ends, using yarn tails at base of fingers and thumbs to close any gaps. Block lightly if desired. Cut two lengths of ¼" (6 mm) ribbon about 1¼ yd (114.5 cm) long. Beg and ending at center of the Chevron chart patt, weave a ribbon through the eyelet rnd in the lace border at the top of each glove, then tie in a bow as shown. ❧

HEATHER ZOPPETTI lives in Lancaster, Pennsylvania, with her husband and yarn collection. She can be found online at hzoppettidesigns.com.

Pemberley Reticule

CATHERINE SALTER BAYAR

Reticule is an old term for a small handbag, which alludes to the fact that they were originally made of netted fabric—Latin *rete,* meaning net, became *reticulum,* or netted bag. Knitted as gifts for sisters and friends, rarely for themselves, women would only be able to carry a few coins in them. Not exactly practical for modern day use, so this larger-than-Regency style scales-up that net to create a bag that goes from market to beach, adding gothic floral-lace motifs, which grace and stabilize the base and top.

FINISHED SIZE About 28" (71 cm) circumference and 19" (48.5 cm) tall, without straps.

YARN DK weight (#3 Light)
Shown here: KnitPicks CotLin (70% Tanguis cotton, 30% linen; 123 yd [112 m]/1 3/5 oz [50 g]): loden, 7 skeins. Distributed by Crafts Americana.

NEEDLES Size 7 (4.5 mm), Size 6 (4 mm), Size 5 (3.75 mm) and Size 4 (3.5 mm) circular (cir), and Size 7 (4.5 mm) set of 5 double-pointed (dpn). Adjust needle size if necessary to obtain the correct gauge.

NOTIONS Tapestry needle, markers (m), stitch holder.

GAUGE 21 sts and 28 rows = 5" (12.5 cm) in St st with Size 7 (4.5 mm) needles with yarn held double: 21 st and 24 rows = 4" (10 cm) in St st with Size 5 (3.75 mm) needles.

Notes

- *Worked from the bottom up in the round, descending needle sizes shape the bag without decreasing stitches. Needle size can be varied to make the bag looser or more structured, as desired.*

- *The yarn is doubled at the bottom to make it sturdier.*

BAG

With Size 7 dpn and yarn held double, CO 12 sts, distribute 3 sts to each of 4 needles, pm and join in the rnd. Work Rnds 1–36 of Base Leaf chart on each of the 4 needles, switching to Size 7 cir when possible—152 sts.

Inc rnd: [Yo, k2tog] 18 times, [yo, k1] 2 times, ★yo, k2tog; rep from ★ to end of rnd—154 sts.

Next rnd: ★Yo, k2tog; rep from ★ to end. Rep last rnd with yarn held double until the bag measures 8" (20.5 cm) from the bottom center.

Change to Size 6 cir and a single strand of yarn. Cont in patt until bag measures 11½" (29 cm) from bottom center.

Lace Top

Change to Size 5 cir and work Rnds 1–12 of Gothic Arch Lace chart 2 times. Change to Size 4 needles and rep Rnds 1–12 of chart once, then work Rnds 13–20—140 sts rem after chart complete.

Ribbing

Cont with Size 4 cir, work in k1, p1 rib as established for 1½" (3.8 cm).

STRAPS

Next rnd: With Size 5 cir, BO 15 sts in patt, work 21 sts in patt and place on holder for first strap, BO 49 sts in patt, work 21 sts in patt and place on holder for second strap, BO rem sts in patt. ★Attach yarn to base of 21 sts on holder

for strap. With Size 5 cir, work in k1, p1 rib until the strap measures 20" (51 cm). Work Rows 1–27 of Gothic Arch Strap End chart. BO rem 5 sts. Rep from ★ for second strap.

FINISHING

Weave in loose ends, closing the hole at center bottom. Block bag to measurements. Knot straps at shoulder. 🍂

California native **CATHERINE SALTER BAYAR** is a clothing, interiors, and knitwear designer who relocated to Turkey in 1999 to pursue her love of handmade textiles and fiber arts. Bazaar Bayar is a handcrafts workshop she founded in Istanbul to provide work to local artisans and to teach visiting women about Turkish handcrafts—both traditional and modern. Learn more at bazaarbayar.com.

"It is amazing to me," said Bingley, "how young ladies can have patience to be so very accomplished as they all are.... They all paint tables, cover screens, and net purses. I scarcely know anyone who cannot do all this, and I am sure I never heard a young lady spoken of for the first time, without being informed that she was very accomplished."

—*Pride and Prejudice*

Base Leaf Chart

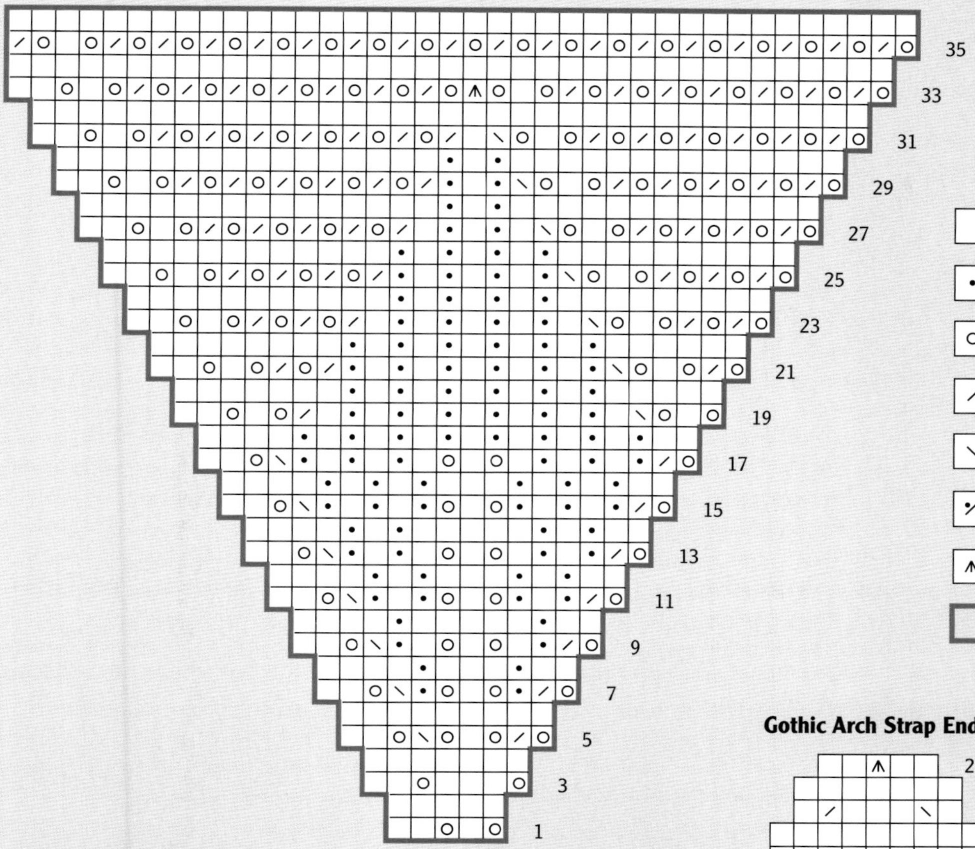

35
33
31
29
27
25
23
21
19
17
15
13
11
9
7
5
3
1

3 to 38 st repeat

Legend

☐	k on RS, p on WS
•	p on RS, k on WS
○	yo
╱	k2tog
╲	ssk
⟋	p2tog
⋀	sl 2 as if to k2tog, k1, p2sso
☐	pattern repeat

Gothic Arch Lace Chart

19
17
15
13
11
9
7
5
3
1

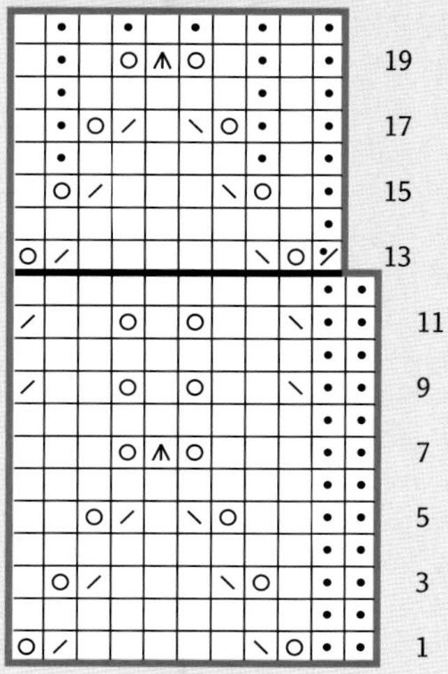

11 dec'd to 10 st repeat

Gothic Arch Strap End Chart

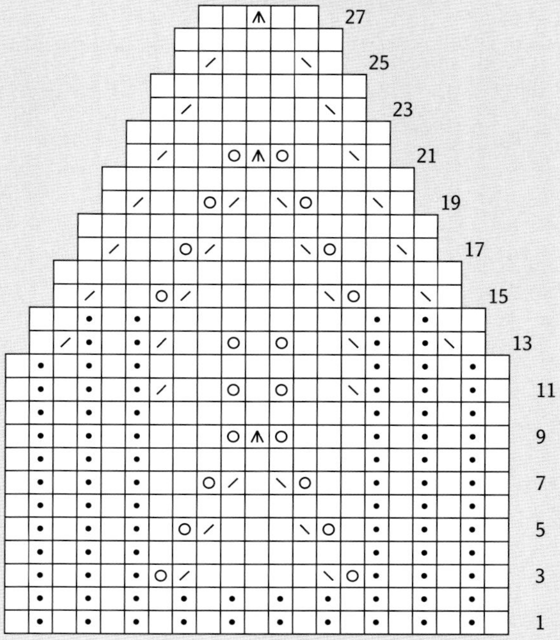

27
25
23
21
19
17
15
13
11
9
7
5
3
1

21 dec'd to 5 sts

Dressmaking
in JANE AUSTEN'S
TIME

BY SUE FORGUE

Jane Austen's lifetime, a period variously referred to in fashion history as the Regency era, the late Georgian era, or the vertical epoch, is widely considered to be an age of elegance and ease of wear in women's clothes. This is especially true in view of what was fashionable immediately before, in the late eighteenth century, with the obscenely wide hoops and what would follow, beginning in the 1820s, with increasingly more restrictive corsets. But other than mentions of visiting a warehouse, the acquisition of a new frock is hardly discussed in Austen's novels. Thankfully, there are more mentions in her letters to her sister, Cassandra, where we can gather more information.

Most of the time, because fabrics were expensive, especially fabrics smuggled because of the Napoleonic Wars such as French silk or lace, ladies recycled their clothing by changing the trimmings, dyeing their dresses, or even taking them apart and reconfiguring them to the current fashion. Yet there were some times when buying new clothing was advisable, even expected, and not to do so was a serious social faux pas. These included updating one's wardrobe on first arriving in Bath or London in advance of the Season, or assembling one's trousseau, as illustrated by Mrs. Bennet bewailing the lack of wedding clothes for Lydia in *Pride and Prejudice*.

The Linendraper bold

An Illustration by Randolph Caldecott from William Cowper's book *The Diverting History of John Gilpin*, published in 1881, depicting a young woman from the earlier Regency era shopping at the linen drapers. A draper was equivalent to today's wholesaler of cloth, mainly for clothing.

If traveling to a warehouse to pick out clothes sounds a bit weird to our ears today, the reality is that the word warehouse had a much more literal meaning then. None of Austen's female characters would venture to an industrial area to shop among the crates. A warehouse two hundred years ago meant a large shop or emporium with merchandise frequently not made on the shop's premises such as fabrics, threads, buttons, trimmings, etc. But even with that definition, these ladies would not buy their dresses off the rack as we do today. Ready-made garments were not generally available except on the secondhand market and sold in places Jane Austen or her characters would never visit.

The dress materials mentioned are the same items that you'd expect to find in any good fabric store today, with one glaring omission: dress patterns. Printed paper patterns were very rare. Of the many publications catering to women only, *The Lady's Magazine* (published 1770–1819), contained fold-out patterns in its issues, but these were usually removed by readers of the time and most are now lost. Without paper patterns, one used an old garment that was worn beyond repair or copied someone else's outfit to make what was called a pattern dress.

While there were only four natural fibers in use then—wool, silk, linen, and cotton—there were a large number of woven structures, so that there were many finished fabrics to choose from. The Napoleonic Wars had a major impact on fashion as French silk was officially banned until 1826, and wool cloth was needed for uniforms. Cotton textiles, originally woven in India and then later woven in England, were

"We are very busy making Edward's shirts, and I am proud to say that I am the neatest worker of the party."

Jane Austen,
September 1796

readily available and cheaper. This is why day dresses made of muslin, cambric, and calico became the most used fabrics, even in wintertime. Jane Austen was also very interested in the fabrics she picked for her frocks as she writes to her sister on January 25, 1801: "I shall want two new coloured gowns for the summer, for my pink one will not do more than clear me for Steventon. I shall not trouble you, however, to get more than one of them, and that is to be a plain cambric muslin, for morning wear; the other, which is to be a very pretty yellow and white cloud, I mean to buy in Bath." But the yearning for French silk wasn't interrupted for long by the inability to legally purchase it. Despite the heavy criminal penalties for smuggling, luxury goods such as silk and lace soon found their way back into high society. Along with an Italian silk called sarcenet, French silk was increasingly used for evening and court dress.

How much fabric to purchase was naturally determined by the wearer's

size and the fashion of the day. In the same letter dated January 25, Austen instructs her sister to purchase dress lengths of "seven yards for my mother, seven yards and a half for me." Once laden with the fabric and all the trimmings, the next decision to be made was who was going to sew up the dress. Unlike today, when finished goods are less expensive than the labor used in the making of them, in the Regency era, hiring someone to make the dress was not the major expenditure; buying the cloth was.

Of course, the wearer or her servant could complete the dress. Women of all classes were expected to know how to make their own clothing, their family's wardrobe, and garments for the poor. All of this sewing was referred to as "work" and is illustrated first by Mrs. Norris pompously chiding Fanny Price in *Mansfield Park,* "If you have no work of your own, I can supply you from the poor basket." And then there is this quote from Mrs. Morland in *Northanger Abbey*: ". . . but there is a time for everything—a time for balls and plays, and a time for work." Women would make or repair articles of clothing when they were with relatives or close friends. Decorative embroidery or lacemaking would be the appropriate "work" when company came to visit.

The clothing that women made at home would include not only dresses for themselves and their daughters but shirts and cravats for the menfolk of the family, baby clothes, and underwear and handkerchiefs for both genders. Jane Austen was not exempt from that expectation as she proudly tells her sister in a letter of September 1, 1796, "We are very busy making Edward's

·The 3 Customers

Another illustration by Randolph Caldecott from *The Diverting History of John Gilpin,* depicting a group of Regency ladies in the high street.

shirts, and I am proud to say that I am the neatest worker of the party."

Most ladies of the gentry and aristocracy would have visited their favorite dressmaker, called a modiste. Rarely, there is a mention of a mantua-maker, which is the older term for a dressmaker (a mantua is an earlier eighteenth-century gown). The one

shopping exception would be for the acquisition of a riding habit. Since riding habits were based on men's styling, many men's tailors as well as dressmakers made them.

Austen mentions two visits to acquire her completed dresses. While she does not label these women as modistes, it's clear from these quotes that they

are some sort of dressmaker. The first quote is from a November 20, 1800, letter to her sister: "Miss Summers has made my gown very well indeed, & I grow more & more pleased with it." The second citation is from a letter dated May 27, 1801, also to Cassandra. "I will engage Mrs. Mussell as you desire. She made my dark gown very well &

may be trusted I hope with Yours—but she does not always succeed with lighter Colours. My white one I was obliged to alter a good deal." From these quotes, it's quite clear that there were choices available, and there was concern about the work done.

At the modiste's shop, fashion prints and, if she was artistically inclined, the modiste's own sketches would be on display for inspiration. One could also purchase fabric and trimmings while there, but there were further options to be considered, mostly depending on one's budget. To save money, the modiste could be hired just to cut the fabric into dress pieces. It was expected that the modiste would know how to cut the cloth so there was the least amount of wasted fabric. Another option for more cost was for the modiste to cut the fabric and baste the dress pieces together. This allowed the wearer or her servant to complete all the fine seams and add the decoration.

But whoever made the dress, every single one was entirely handstitched. There was a sewing machine patented by Thomas Saint in England in 1790, but it was only used for stitching leather and canvas, and it was never advertised for sale. Sewing machines in general use would not be common until at least four decades later. In Austen's time, a very experienced seamstress could sew thirty stitches a minute, a very slow speed compared to our modern sewing machines, but rapid enough that a dress could be completed within a week and even less than that if there were other seamstresses on staff.

Despite the difficulties in acquiring a new dress, there were many seamstresses in the major cities, and every village would have at least one dressmaker, if only to capitalize on the local gentry ladies' immediate clothing needs. Georgian ladies were very fashion aware, and Jane Austen was just as dress conscious. But as she was in a state of genteel poverty for most of her adult life, she gave her heroines the indulgence of new wardrobes. She writes about Catherine Morland and her chaperone, Mrs. Allen, in *Northanger Abbey* on their arrival in Bath: ". . . our heroine's entrée into life could not take place till after three or four days had been spent in learning what was mostly worn, and her chaperone was provided with a dress of the newest fashion."

Jane Austen Society of North America life member, Chicago chapter board member, and an accountant by trade, SUE FORGUE is also the creator and Webmistress of the research website, The Regency Encyclopedia (regency.com—User ID: JAScholar, Password: Academia—both case sensitive). As an enthusiastic admirer of Jane Austen's writings and a history buff, she loves uncovering insights into Jane Austen's characters by the historical details that can be mined in the novels.

An Aran for Frederick

KATHLEEN DAMES

Though Captain Frederick Wentworth may not be Irish, this handsome captain, who stole Anne Elliot's heart before the beginning of Jane Austen's *Persuasion,* is certainly worthy of his own Aran sweater. This cabled pullover features a Celtic flourish cable running up the center back and front, flanked by OXO and superimposed double wave cables, and Ensign's Braids (ensigns were junior officers in the infantry and navy at the time) running up the sleeves and along the shoulders. It is finished with a simple rolled neck so as not to distract from this cable tour de force.

FINISHED SIZE 37¼ (43½, 49, 53¼, 59½)" (94.5 [110.5, 124.5, 135.5, 151] cm) chest circumference. Sweater shown measures 43½" (110.5 cm).

YARN Worsted weight (#4 Medium) *Shown here:* Brooklyn Tweed Shelter (100% wool; 140 yd [128 m]/1 ¾ oz [50 g]): #16 nest, 8 (10, 12, 14, 15) skeins.

NEEDLES Size 6 (4 mm): 16" (40.5 cm) and 29" (73.5 cm) circular (cir) and set of double-pointed (dpn). Adjust needle size if necessary to obtain the correct gauge.

NOTIONS Markers (m); cable needle (cn); locking markers; stitch holders or waste yarn; tapestry needle.

GAUGE 15 sts and 27 rnds = 4" (10 cm) in seed st; 18 sts of Double Wave chart = 3½" (9 cm); 10 sts of OXO chart = 2" (5 cm); 28 sts of Celtic Flourish chart = 6" (15 cm); 22 sts of Ensign's Braid chart = 2½" (6.5 cm).

Notes

- Cabling without a cable needle is brilliant.
- Spit splicing this yarn works like a dream, and will almost eliminate ends to weave in.
- Front and back stitch counts do not include increased stitches on Rows 8–22 of Celtic Flourish chart and Back Saddle chart.

BODY

With longer cir needle, CO 180 (204, 224, 240, 264) sts. Place marker and join in the rnd.

Next rnd: Beg and ending each chart as indicated for your size, work 3 (9, 9, 13, 19) sts in seed st (see Stitch Guide), pm, work Double Wave chart over 18 (18, 20, 20, 20) sts, pm, work OXO chart over 10 (10, 12, 12, 12) sts, pm, work Celtic Flourish chart over 28 (28, 30, 30, 30) sts, pm, work OXO chart over 10 (10, 12, 12, 12) sts, pm, work Double Wave chart over 18 (18, 20, 20, 20) sts, pm, work 3 (9, 9, 13, 19) sts in seed st, pm for side, cont in seed st over 3 (9, 9, 13, 19) sts, pm, work Double Wave chart over 18 (18, 20, 20, 20) sts, pm, work OXO chart over 10 (10, 12, 12, 12) sts, pm, work Celtic Flourish chart over 28 (28, 30, 30, 30) sts, pm, work OXO chart over 10 (10, 12, 12, 12) sts, pm, work Double Wave chart over 18 (18, 20, 20, 20) sts, pm, work 3 (9, 9, 13, 19) sts in seed st. Cont in patt until piece measures 16 (17, 17½, 17½,

18)" (40.5 [43, 44.5, 44.5, 45.5] cm) from CO, ending with an even-numbered rnd.

Next rnd: Work 86 (97, 106, 114, 125) sts in patt, place next 8 (10, 12, 12, 14) sts on holder (removing m), work 82 (92, 100, 108, 118) sts in patt, place next 8 (10, 12, 12, 14) sts on holder (removing m)—164 (184, 200, 216, 236) sts rem for body. Break yarn and set aside.

SLEEVES

With dpn, CO 44 (52, 58, 62, 66) sts. Place marker and join in the rnd. Work 1 (5, 5, 7, 9) st(s) in seed st, pm, work OXO chart over 10 (10, 12, 12, 12) sts, pm, work Ensign's Braid chart over 22 (22, 24, 24, 24) sts, pm, work OXO chart over 10 (10, 12, 12, 12) sts, pm, work 1 (5, 5, 7, 9) st(s) in seed st. Work 5 rnds in patt.

Inc rnd: Work 0 (1, 1, 1, 1) st(s) in seed st as established, M1L (see Glossary), work in patt to last 0 (1, 1, 1, 1) st(s), M1R (see Glossary), work 0 (1, 1, 1, 1) st(s) in

seed st—46 (54, 60, 64, 68) sts. Work 5 rnds in patt, working new sts into seed st patt.

Inc rnd: Work 1 st in seed st, M1L, work in patt to last st, M1R, work 1 st in seed st—2 sts inc'd. Rep last 6 rnds 4 (5, 6, 8, 9) more times—56 (66, 74, 82, 88) sts. Work even until piece measures 17½ (18, 19, 19½, 20)" (44.5 [45.5, 48.5, 49.5, 51] cm) from CO, ending with an even-numbered rnd.

Next rnd: Work 52 (61, 68, 76, 81) sts, place next 8 (10, 12, 12, 14) sts on holder (removing m)—48 (56, 62, 70, 74) sts rem. Break yarn and set aside, placing first sleeve on shorter cir needle and leaving 2nd sleeve on dpn in preparation for joining sleeves to body.

YOKE

With longer needle and cont in patt, work 48 (56, 62, 70, 74) sts of first sleeve, work 82 (92, 100, 108, 118) back sts, placing locking m in first and last st of back, work 48 (56, 62, 70, 74) sleeve

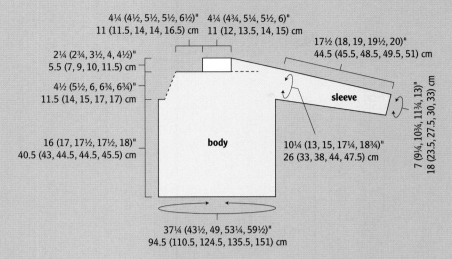

4¼ (4½, 5½, 5½, 6½)"
11 (11.5, 14, 14, 16.5) cm

4¼ (4¾, 5¼, 5½, 6)"
11 (12, 13.5, 14, 15) cm

17½ (18, 19, 19½, 20)"
44.5 (45.5, 48.5, 49.5, 51) cm

2¼ (2¾, 3½, 4, 4½)"
5.5 (7, 9, 10, 11.5) cm

4½ (5½, 6, 6¾, 6¾)"
11.5 (14, 15, 17, 17) cm

sleeve

7 (9¼, 10¾, 11¾, 13)"
18 (23.5, 27.5, 30, 33) cm

16 (17, 17½, 17½, 18)"
40.5 (43, 44.5, 44.5, 45.5) cm

body

10¼ (13, 15, 17¼, 18¾)"
26 (33, 38, 44, 47.5) cm

37¼ (43½, 49, 53¼, 59½)"
94.5 (110.5, 124.5, 135.5, 151) cm

☐	k on RS; p on WS
•	p on RS; k on WS
MR	M1R (see Glossary)
ML	M1L (see Glossary)
⋁	(k1, p1, k1) in same st
⌂	4-st dec (see Stitch Guide)
▨	no stitch

sl 1 st onto cn, hold in back, k2, p1 from cn

sl 2 sts onto cn, hold in front, p1, k2 from cn

sl 1 st onto cn, hold in back, k3, p1 from cn

sl 3 sts onto cn, hold in front, p1, k3 from cn

sl 2 sts onto cn, hold in back, k2, p2 from cn

sl 2 sts onto cn, hold in front, p2, k2 from cn

sl 2 sts onto cn, hold in back, k2, k2 from cn

sl 2 sts onto cn, hold in front, k2, k2 from cn

sl 3 sts onto cn, hold in back, k2, sl last st
from cn to left needle, p1, k2 from cn

sl 3 sts onto cn, hold in back, k3, k3 from cn

sl 3 sts onto cn, hold in front, k3, k3 from cn

Double Wave Chart

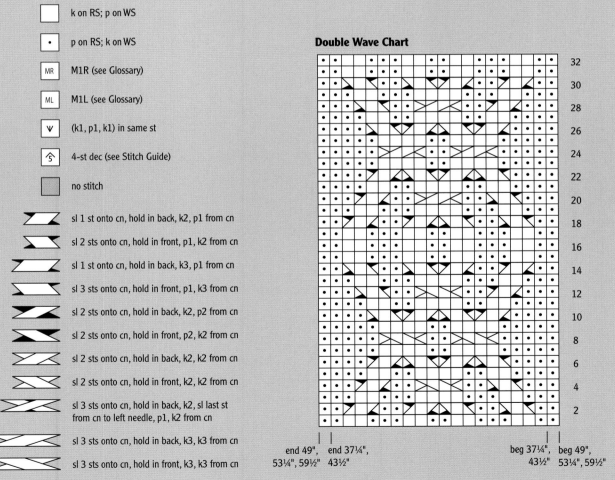

32
30
28
26
24
22
20
18
16
14
12
10
8
6
4
2

end 49",
53¼", 59½"

end 37¼",
43½"

beg 37¼",
43½"

beg 49",
53¼", 59½"

Celtic Flourish Chart

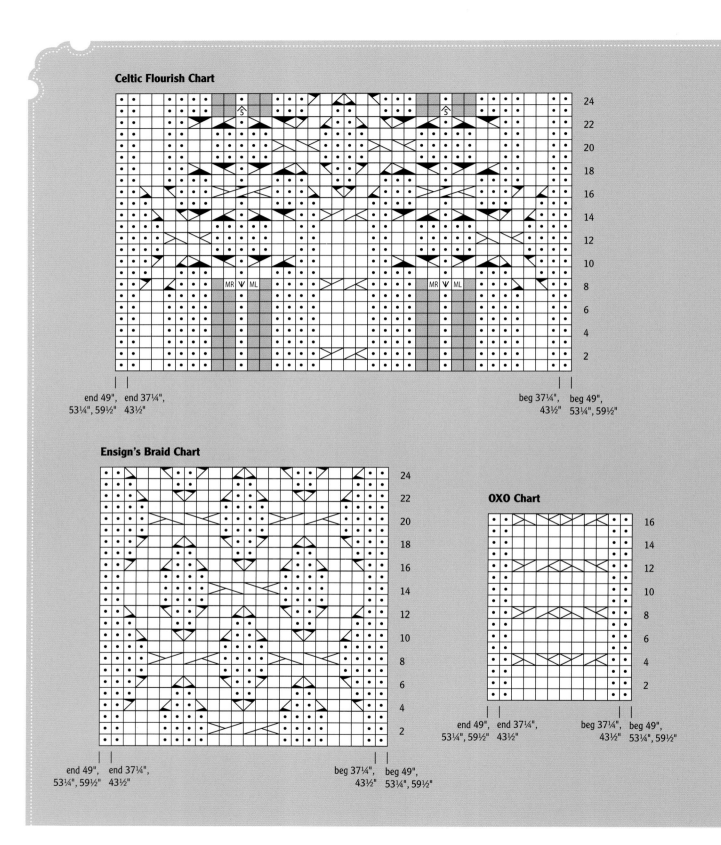

24
22
20
18
16
14
12
10
8
6
4
2

end 49", end 37¼",
53¼", 59½" 43½"

beg 37¼", beg 49",
43½" 53¼", 59½"

Ensign's Braid Chart

24
22
20
18
16
14
12
10
8
6
4
2

end 49", end 37¼",
53¼", 59½" 43½"

beg 37¼", beg 49",
43½" 53¼", 59½"

OXO Chart

16
14
12
10
8
6
4
2

end 49", end 37¼",
53¼", 59½" 43½"

beg 37¼", beg 49",
43½" 53¼", 59½"

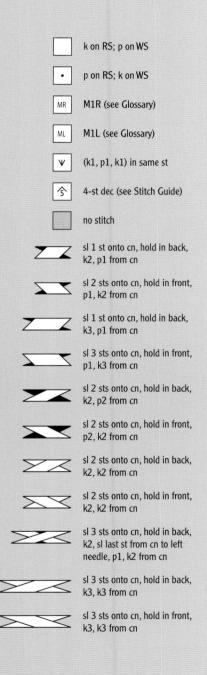

	k on RS; p on WS
·	p on RS; k on WS
MR	M1R (see Glossary)
ML	M1L (see Glossary)
V	(k1, p1, k1) in same st
⌃S	4-st dec (see Stitch Guide)
	no stitch
	sl 1 st onto cn, hold in back, k2, p1 from cn
	sl 2 sts onto cn, hold in front, p1, k2 from cn
	sl 1 st onto cn, hold in back, k3, p1 from cn
	sl 3 sts onto cn, hold in front, p1, k3 from cn
	sl 2 sts onto cn, hold in back, k2, p2 from cn
	sl 2 sts onto cn, hold in front, p2, k2 from cn
	sl 2 sts onto cn, hold in back, k2, k2 from cn
	sl 2 sts onto cn, hold in front, k2, k2 from cn
	sl 3 sts onto cn, hold in back, k2, sl last st from cn to left needle, p1, k2 from cn
	sl 3 sts onto cn, hold in back, k3, k3 from cn
	sl 3 sts onto cn, hold in front, k3, k3 from cn

"A well-looking man," said Sir Walter, "a very well-looking man." "A very fine young man indeed!" said Lady Dalrymple. "More air than one often sees in Bath. Irish, I dare say." "No. I just know his name. A bowing acquaintance. Wentworth— Captain Wentworth of the navy."

—Persuasion

sts, work 82 (92, 100, 108, 118) front sts, placing locking m in first and last st of front, pm for beg of rnd—260 (296, 324, 356, 384) sts total. Work 2 rnds even in patt.

Dec rnd: ★Work to 1 st before marked st, s2kp2; rep from ★ 3 more times, removing end-of-rnd m to work last s2kp2 and replacing after dec—8 sts dec'd.

Note: When marked sts are incorporated into cables, move m to new st in marked position.

Rep last 3 rnds 9 (11, 12, 14, 14) more times—180 (200, 220, 236, 264) sts rem: 62 (68, 74, 78, 88) sts for each of front and back, 28 (32, 36, 40, 44) sts for each sleeve. If final dec rnd is an even rnd, work an odd rnd. Make note of last row worked on Celtic Flourish chart.

Right Shoulder Saddle

Work back and forth over 28 (32, 36, 40, 44) sleeve sts plus 1 marked st at each edge of sleeve—30 (34, 38, 42, 46) sts total.

Next row: (RS) P3 (5, 6, 8, 10), cont Ensign's Braid chart over 22 (22, 24, 24, 24) sts, p3 (5, 6, 8, 10), ssk (marked st and next st from back), turn.

Next row: (WS) Sl 1 pwise with yarn in front (wyf), k3 (5, 6, 8, 10), cont chart over 22 (22, 24, 24, 24) sts, k3 (5, 6, 8, 10), p2tog (marked st and next st from front), turn.

Next row: (RS) Sl 1 kwise with yarn in back (wyb), p3 (5, 6, 8, 10), cont chart over 22 (22, 24, 24, 24) sts, p3 (5, 6, 8, 10), ssk (last st from saddle and next st from back), turn. Rep last 2 rows 18 (20, 22, 23, 27) more times, then work WS row once more—40 (44, 48, 51, 57) sts rem for each of front and back, excluding marked sts. Break yarn.

Left Shoulder Saddle

With RS facing, sl 70 (78, 86, 93, 103) sts to arrive at marked st before left sleeve.

Next row: (RS) Sl 1 kwise wyb, p3 (5, 6, 8, 10), cont Ensign's Braid chart over 22 (22, 24, 24, 24) sts, p3 (5, 6, 8, 10), ssk (last st from saddle and next st from front), turn.

Next row: (WS) Sl 1 pwise with yarn in front (wyf), k3 (5, 6, 8, 10), cont chart over 22 (22, 24, 24, 24) sts, k3 (5, 6, 8, 10), p2tog (marked st and next st from back), turn. Rep last 2 rows 19 (21, 23, 24, 28) more times—20 (22, 24, 26, 28) sts rem for each of front and back, excluding marked sts. Break yarn.

Back Saddle

With WS facing, sl 20 (22, 24, 26, 28) sts to arrive at marked st of right sleeve; turn. Work back and forth over 20 (22, 24, 26, 28) back sts, beg Back Saddle chart on row after last row worked of Celtic Flourish chart.

Note: If you will not complete Row 23 of Back Saddle chart in the course of the back saddle (there are 28 [32, 36, 40, 44] total back saddle rows), do not work increases on Row 8 and maintain center cable instead, working rem sts on each side in rev St st (purl on RS, knit on WS).

Next row: (RS) Sl 1 kwise wyb, work Back Saddle chart to last st, ssk (last st from back saddle and next st from left sleeve saddle), turn.

Next row: (WS) Sl 1 pwise wyf, work Back Saddle chart to last st, p2tog (last st from back saddle and next st from right sleeve saddle), turn. Rep last 2 rows 13 (15, 17, 19, 21) more times—16 (18, 20, 22, 24) sts rem for each sleeve.

Neck

With shorter cir needle and RS facing, sl 1 pwise wyb, k18 (20, 22, 24, 26), ssk, k14 (16, 18, 20, 22), ssk, k18 (20, 22, 24, 26), k2tog, k14 (16, 18, 20, 22), k2tog (last st of rnd and first st of rnd)—68 (76, 84, 92, 100) sts rem. Knit 12 rnds. Using the k2tog tbl method (see Stitch Guide), BO all sts.

FINISHING

Graft held sts at underarm tog using Kitchener st (see Glossary). Weave in loose ends and block. ❧

KATHLEEN DAMES designs and knits in New York City and Bath, Maine, with her very own Captain Wentworth and their three children. All of Jane Austen's works have provided her with joy and inspiration. You can find more of Kathleen's designs at kathleendames.blogspot.com, and she goes by the username Purly on Ravelry.

Back Saddle Chart

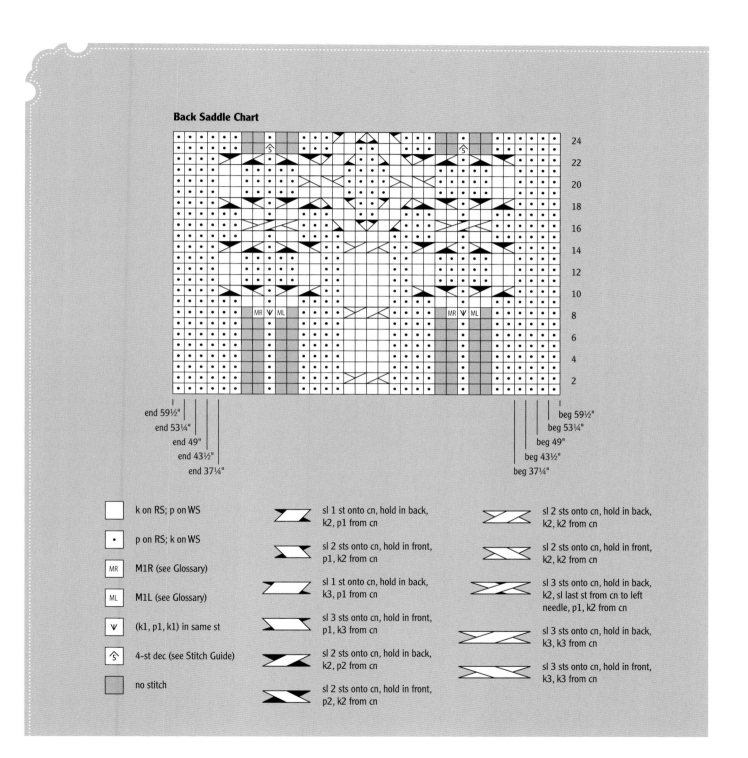

24
22
20
18
16
14
12
10
8
6
4
2

end 59½"
end 53¼"
end 49"
end 43½"
end 37¼"

beg 59½"
beg 53¼"
beg 49"
beg 43½"
beg 37¼"

☐ k on RS; p on WS	
• p on RS; k on WS	
MR M1R (see Glossary)	
ML M1L (see Glossary)	
V (k1, p1, k1) in same st	
⤺ 4-st dec (see Stitch Guide)	
▨ no stitch	

sl 1 st onto cn, hold in back, k2, p1 from cn

sl 2 sts onto cn, hold in front, p1, k2 from cn

sl 1 st onto cn, hold in back, k3, p1 from cn

sl 3 sts onto cn, hold in front, p1, k3 from cn

sl 2 sts onto cn, hold in back, k2, p2 from cn

sl 2 sts onto cn, hold in front, p2, k2 from cn

sl 2 sts onto cn, hold in back, k2, k2 from cn

sl 2 sts onto cn, hold in front, k2, k2 from cn

sl 3 sts onto cn, hold in back, k2, sl last st from cn to left needle, p1, k2 from cn

sl 3 sts onto cn, hold in back, k3, k3 from cn

sl 3 sts onto cn, hold in front, k3, k3 from cn

Love & Loyalty Pin Ball

ANNE CARROLL GILMOUR

This little project is typical of the pin balls often produced as gifts for dear friends by schoolgirls and ladies of the Regency period. They used personalized medallion-like symbols (often derived from printed motifs for embroidery samplers) to represent love, unity, loyalty, joy, devotion, and other concepts. Anne Carroll Gilmour's version consists of two charted pieces knitted flat in two-color intarsia technique, then stuffed and sewn together in the traditional manner with a ribbon or twisted rope trim (your choice) whipstitched in place to cover the seam.

FINISHED SIZE About 2" (5 cm) in diameter and 6¼" (16 cm) circumference, after finishing.

YARN Crochet thread (#0 Lace) *Shown here:* DMC Cébélia Crochet Cotton Size 20 (100% cotton; 415 yd [379 m]/1¾ oz [50 g]): #0799 horizon blue (A), #0437 camel (B), and #0712 cream (C), 1 ball each.

NEEDLES Size 0000 (1.25 mm). Adjust needle size if necessary to obtain the correct gauge.

NOTIONS Two cardboard circles 2" (5 cm) diameter; small tapestry needle; small amount of lambswool or polyester fiberfill for stuffing; optional 30" (76 cm) purchased braid or ribbon (or make twisted cord as shown here).

GAUGE 17 sts and 19 rows = 1" (2.5 cm) in St st colorwork patts from charts.

Note

• *The charts are worked in a combination of intarsia and stranded stockinette. The main color is used all the way across each row, but the contrasting color is only used for the pattern area. Work each row with the main color to the start of the pattern, use both colors to work the pattern in stranded stockinette, then work with the main color only to the end of the row.*

LOVE AND LOYALTY PANEL

With A and using the long-tail method, CO 33 sts. Work WS set-up row of Love and Loyalty chart, then work Rows 1–53, ending with a RS row. BO all sts leaving a 20" (51 cm) tail for gathering edges.

ROOTS AND WINGS PANEL

With B and using the long-tail method, CO 34 sts. Work WS set-up row of Roots and Wings chart, then work Rows 1–53, ending with a RS row. BO all sts leaving a 20" (51 cm) tail for gathering edges.

FINISHING

Block pieces, if desired.

Assembly

Thread 20" tail on a small tapestry needle and work a running st all around the perimeter of the panel. Leave the needle threaded, and gently pull to begin gathering the edges, forming a small, cupped shape. Stuff the shape tightly, and insert a cardboard circle on top of the stuffing. Pull the gathering thread snug to ensure that the panel is centered firmly around the cardboard. Using the tail still threaded on the tapestry needle, lash the edges of the piece together across the back of the cardboard, and fasten off the tail firmly. Stuff the other panel in the same manner. Place the two halves with their flat cardboard sides together, making sure both patterns are oriented the same way up, or in any arrangement that pleases you, and use mattress stitch to join them.

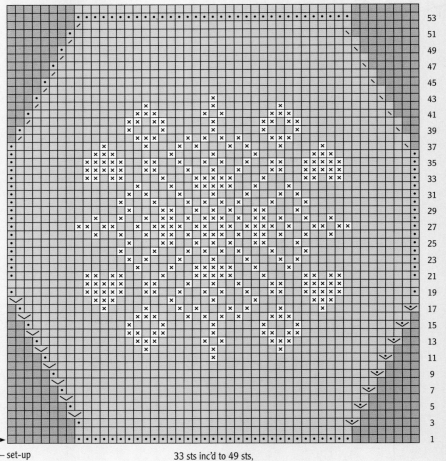

Love and Loyalty Chart

33 sts inc'd to 49 sts, then dec'd to 33 sts

set-up

Wrap purchased ribbon, braid or self-made twisted cord (see below) around the join between the two halves, and use whipstitch to sew it in place, covering the join. If using ribbon, tie in a decorative bow at the top.

Twisted Cord (Optional)

I like to use about 30" (76 cm) of matching twisted cord, tied in an overhand knot at the top of the pin ball, which leaves the ends long enough to attach the pinball to the handles of a basket or loop it around the wrist.

Measure 7 strands of each color 40" (101.5 cm) in length. Tie the 21 strands together at one end with a firm overhand knot. Loop the knotted end over a stationary object, and twist each 7-strand bundle of the same color separately clockwise for 200 complete revolutions—3 twisted bundles. Hold the twisted bundles together and parallel, knot them together at the other end, then allow them to twist back on themselves, guiding the twist evenly along the cord until it is balanced and no longer kinked—30" (76 cm) of cord. Trim the ends even beyond the knots.

ANNE CARROLL GILMOUR never recovered from a magical childhood in historic Williamsburg, Virginia. It instilled a particular love for the Regency era and the traditional knitting and other textile techniques she has used for decades. She now lives in the beautiful Wasatch Mountains near Park City, Utah, where she works in her studio and teaches workshops in spinning, weaving, and knitting. Many of her knitwear patterns are available at wildwestwoolies.com.

Roots and Wings Chart

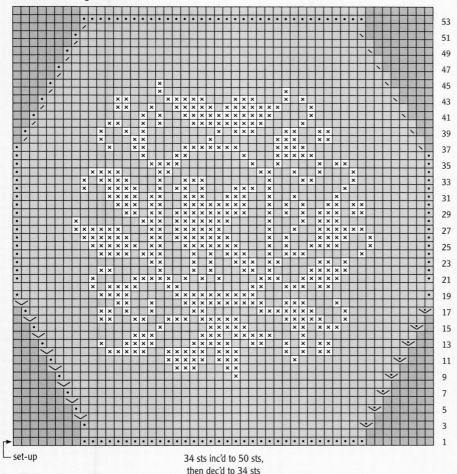

set-up

34 sts inc'd to 50 sts,
then dec'd to 34 sts

Georgiana Shawlette

SUSANNA IC

Fashionable women of the Regency period favored sheer gowns in white and pale pastels. The necklines of their evening dresses were often cut quite low in the French fashion to highlight the chest area, and young British women would use diaphanous scarves trimmed with delicate lace to tuck into their bodices and cover their shoulders in the more modest British style. Georgiana, named for Mr. Darcy's beautiful younger sister in *Pride and Prejudice,* is worked in colorful fingering-weight yarn for a modern twist.

FINISHED SIZE About 36" (91.5 cm) wide at neck edge, 100" (254 cm) wide at lower edge, and 16" (40.5 cm) tall at center point.

YARN Fingering weight (#1 Super Fine) *Shown here:* Madelinetosh Tosh Sock (100% superwash Merino wool; 395 yd [361 m]/3 ½ oz [100 g]): grove, 2 skeins.

NEEDLES Sizes 8, 9, and 10 (5, 5.5, and 6 mm): 32" (81.5 cm) circular (cir). Adjust needle sizes if necessary to obtain the correct gauge.

NOTIONS Tapestry needle; blocking pins; markers (optional).

GAUGE 14 sts and 35 rows = 4" (10 cm) in St st on smallest needle, after blocking.

SHAWLETTE

With largest needle, loosely CO 368 sts. Do not join. Change to middle-size needle.

Rows 1 and 2: Purl.

Row 3: (RS) ★K2tog, yo; rep from ★ to last 2 sts, k2tog—367 sts rem.

Rows 4–6: Purl.

Change to smallest needle. Work Rows 1–22 of Lower Border A chart—211 sts rem. Work Rows 1–16 of Lower Border B chart. Shape shawl using short-rows as foll:

Note: *Do not wrap st before turning.*

Row 1: K110, turn.

Row 2: Sl 1, p8, turn.

Row 3: Sl 1, k7, ssk, k3, turn.

Row 4: Sl 1, p10, p2tog, p3, turn.

Row 5: Sl 1, k13, ssk, k3, turn.

Row 6: Sl 1, p16, p2tog, p3, turn.

Row 7: Sl 1, k19, ssk, k3, turn.

Row 8: Sl 1, p22, p2tog, p3, turn.

Cont short-rows as established, working 3 more sts on each row before working ssk, or p2tog, then work 3 sts after dec before turning, work 42 more short-rows, ending with a WS row—163 sts rem.

Next row: (RS) Sl 1, k151, ssk, k4, turn.

Next row: Sl 1, p155, p2tog, p4, turn—161 sts rem; no sts rem unworked at end of row. Work Rows 1–10 of Upper Border chart.

Upper Edge

Rows 1 and 2: Purl.

Row 3: (RS) ★K2tog, yo; rep from ★ to last st, k1.

Rows 4 and 5: Knit.

With WS facing, BO as foll: ★K2tog, return st to left needle; rep from ★ to end.

FINISHING

Weave in loose ends. Block piece to measurements and shape as shown in blocking schematic, beg with two short sides, foll by center point, then pinning out rem points along long edge. Piece will relax to finished size measurements. ☙

SUSANNA IC has an extensive background in studio arts and art history, which inspires much of her knitting. Her projects and designs can be found on Ravelry (username zuzusus) and at artqualia.com.

Lower Border A

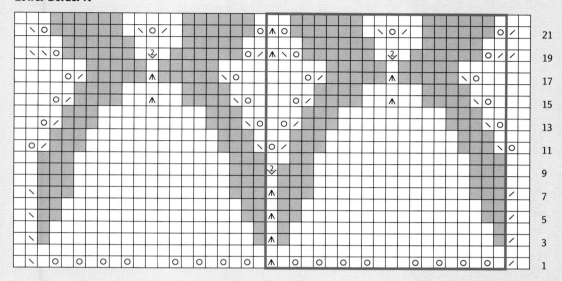

Lower Border B

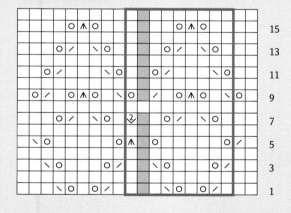

Upper Border

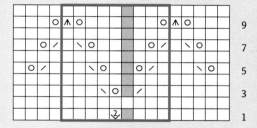

	k on RS; p on WS		∧	sl 2 as if to k2tog, k1, p2sso
○	yo		⊻	(p1, k1) in same st
╱	k2tog			no stitch
╲	ssk			pattern repeat

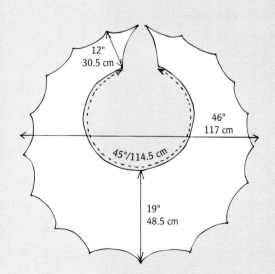

Georgiana Shawlette ◆ **153**

Abbreviations

beg beginning; begin; begins

bet between

BO bind off

CC contrasting color

ch chain

cm centimeter(s)

cn cable needle

CO cast on

cont continue(s); continuing

dc double crochet

dec(s) decrease(s); decreasing

dpn double-pointed needle(s)

foll following; follows

g gram(s)

inc increase(s); increasing

k knit

k1f&b knit into front and back of same st

k2tog knit two stitches together

k3tog knit three stitches together

kwise knitwise

m(s) marker(s)

M1 make one (increase)

MC main color

mm millimeter(s)

p purl

p1f&b purl into front and back of same st

p2tog purl two stitches together

patt(s) pattern(s)

pm place marker

psso pass slipped stitch over

p2sso pass two slipped stitches over

pwise purlwise

rem remain(s); remaining

rep repeat; repeating

rev St st reverse stockinette stitch (purl on RS, knit on WS)

rib ribbing

rnd(s) round(s)

RS right side

sc single crochet

sk skip

Sk2p slip 1 st kwise, k2tog, pass sl st over—2 sts dec'd

sl slip

sl st slip stitch (sl 1 st pwise unless otherwise indicated)

sp space

ssk slip 1 kwise, slip 1 kwise, k2 sl sts tog tbl (decrease)

ssp slip 1 kwise, slip 1 kwise, p2 sl sts tog tbl (decrease)

sssk slip 3 sts kwise individually, then knit them tog tbl—2 sts dec'd

st(s) stitch(es)

St st stockinette stitch (knit on RS, purl on WS)

tbl through back loop

tog together

WS wrong side

wyb with yarn in back

wyf with yarn in front

yo yarn over

* repeat starting point (i.e., repeat from *)

* * repeat all instructions between asterisks

( ) alternate measurements and/or instructions

[ ] instructions that are to be worked as a group a specified number of times

Glossary

BIND-OFF
Three-Needle Bind-Off

Place stitches to be joined onto two separate needles. Hold them with right sides of knitting facing together. Insert a third needle into first stitch on each of the other two needles and knit them together as one stitch.  ★Knit next stitch on each needle the same way. Pass first stitch over second stitch. Repeat from ★ until one stitch remains on third needle. Cut yarn and pull tail through last stitch.

CAST-ONS
Backward-Loop Cast-On

★Loop working yarn and place it on needle backward so that it doesn't unwind. Repeat from ★.

Cable Cast-On

Begin with a slipknot and one knitted cast-on stitch if there are no established stitches. Insert right needle be tween first two stitches on left needle (**Figure 1**). Wrap yarn as if to knit. Draw yarn through to complete stitch (**Figure 2**) and slip this new stitch to left needle as shown (**Figure 3**).

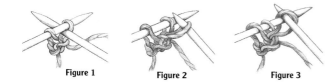

Figure 1   Figure 2   Figure 3

Continental (Long-Tail) Cast-On

Leaving a long tail (about ½" to 1" [1 to 2.5 cm] for each stitch to be cast on), make a slipknot and place on right needle. Place thumb and index finger of left hand between yarn ends so that working yarn is around index finger and tail end is around thumb. Secure ends with your other fin-

gers and hold palm upward, making a V of yarn (**Figure 1**). Bring needle up through loop on thumb (**Figure 2**), grab first strand around index finger with needle, and go back down through loop on thumb (**Figure 3**). Drop loop off thumb and, placing thumb back in V configuration, tighten resulting stitch on needle (**Figure 4**).

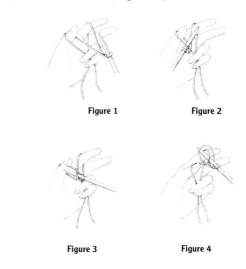

Figure 1   Figure 2

Figure 3   Figure 4

Invisible (Provisional) Cast-On

Place a loose slipknot on needle held in your right hand. Hold waste yarn next to slipknot and around left thumb; hold working yarn over left index finger. ★Bring needle forward under waste yarn, over working yarn, grab a loop of working yarn (**Figure 1**), then bring needle to the front, over both yarns, and grab a second loop (**Figure 2**). Repeat from ★. When you're ready to work in the opposite direction, pick out waste yarn to expose live stitches.

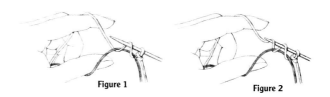

Figure 1   Figure 2

Knitted Cast-On

Place slipknot on left needle if there are no established stitch- es. ★With right needle, knit into first stitch (or slipknot) on left needle (**Figure 1**) and place new stitch onto left needle (**Figure 2**). Repeat from ★, always knitting into last stitch made.

Figure 1   **Figure 2**

CROCHET CHAIN (CH)

Make a slipknot on hook. Yarn over hook and draw it through loop of slipknot. Repeat, drawing yarn through the last loop formed.

DECREASES
K2tog

Knit two stitches together as if they were a single stitch.

K3tog

Knit three stitches together as if they were a single stitch.

P2tog

Purl two stitches together as if they were a single stitch.

Ssk

Slip two stitches individually knitwise (**Figure 1**), insert left needle tip into the front of these two slipped stitches, and use the right needle to knit them together through their back loops (**Figure 2**).

Figure 1   **Figure 2**

Ssp

Holding yarn in front, slip two stitches individually knitwise (**Figure 1**), then slip these two stitches back onto left needle (they will be twisted on the needle), and purl them together through their back loops (**Figure 2**).

Figure 1   **Figure 2**

Sssk

Slip three stitches individually knitwise, insert left needle tip into the front of these three slipped stitches, and use the right needle to knit them together through their back loops.

EMBROIDERY
Duplicate Stitch

Bring threaded needle out from back to front at the base of the V of the knitted stitch you want to cover. ★Working right to left, pass needle in and out under the stitch in the row above it and back into the base of the same stitch. Bring needle back out at the base of the V of the next stitch to the left. Repeat from ★.

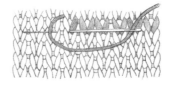

French Knot

Bring needle out of knitted background from back to front, wrap yarn around needle one to three times, and use thumb to hold in place while pulling needle through wraps into background a short distance from where it came out.

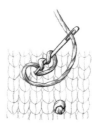

Leaf Stitch

Bring needle out of background from back to front and make a short, diagonal straight stitch. ★Bring needle from back to front just to the left of the straight stitch (**Figure 1**). Insert needle just to right of straight stitch and bring to front, making sure the yarn is lopped under the needle as you pull it through (**Figure 2**). Insert needle under loop and bring to front just to left of stitch (**Figure 3**). Repeat from ★ as many times as desired (**Figure 4**).

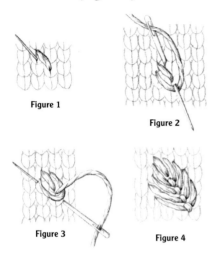

Figure 1

Figure 2

Figure 3

Figure 4

Running Stitch

Working small straight stitches, pass the threaded needle over one knitted stitch and under the next to form a dashed line. The stitches can be worked in equal or varying lengths, horizontally, vertically, or diagonally.

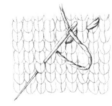

Straight Stitch

★Bring threaded needle out from back to front at base of knitted stitch(es) you want to cover. Insert needle at top of stitch(es) you want to cover. Repeat from ★.

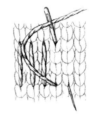

I-CORD

With double-pointed needle, cast on desired number of stitches. ★Without turning the needle, slide the stitches to other end of the needle, pull the yarn around the back, and knit the stitches a usual; repeat from ★ for desired length.

INCREASES
Knitwise Bar Increase

K1f&b: Knit into a stitch but leave the stitch on the left needle (**Figure 1**), then knit through the back loop of the same stitch (**Figure 2**) and slip the original stitch off the needle (**Figure 3**).

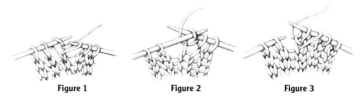

Figure 1   Figure 2   Figure 3

Lifted Increase

Right (RLI): Knit into the back of stitch (in the "purl bump") in the row directly below the stitch on the left needle (**Figure 1**).

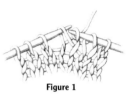

Figure 1

Purl (RLPI): Purl into the stitch in the row directly below the stitch on the left needle.

Left (LLI): Insert left needle into back of the stitch below stitch just knitted (**Figure 2**). Knit this stitch (**Figure 3**).

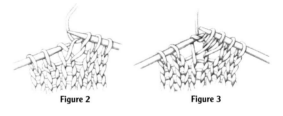

Figure 2   Figure 3

Purl (LLPI): Purl into the stitch below the stitch just purled.

Make One Increases

Make one right (M1R): Insert left needle from back to front under strand of yarn running between last stitch on left needle and first stitch on right needle (**Figure 1**). Knit the lifted strand through its front loop (**Figure 2**)—one stitch increased.

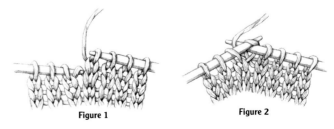

Figure 1   Figure 2

Make one left (M1L): Insert left needle from front to back under strand of yarn running between last stitch on left needle and first stitch on right needle **(Figure 1)**. Knit the lifted strand through its back loop **(Figure 2)**—one stitch increased.

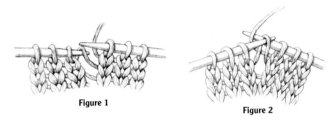

Figure 1   Figure 2

Make one purl (M1P): Insert left needle from back to front under strand of yarn running between last stitch on left needle and first stitch on right needle **(Figure 1)**, then purl the lifted strand through its front loop **(Figure 2)**—one stitch increased.

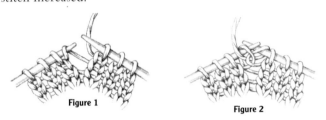

Figure 1   Figure 2

SEAMING
Kitchener Stitch

Step 1: Bring threaded needle through front stitch as if to purl and leave stitch on needle.

Step 2: Bring threaded needle through back stitch as if to knit and leave stitch on needle.

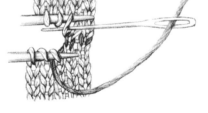

Step 3: Bring threaded needle through first front stitch as if to knit and slip this stitch off needle. Bring threaded needle through next front stitch as if to purl and leave stitch on needle.

Step 4: Bring threaded needle through first back stitch as if to purl (as illustrated), slip this stitch off, bring needle through next back stitch as if to knit, leave this stitch on needle.

Repeat Steps 3 and 4 until no stitches remain on needles.

Mattress-Stitch Seam

With RS of knitting facing, use threaded needle to pick up one bar between first two stitches on one piece **(Figure 1)**, then corresponding bar plus the bar above it on other piece **(Figure 2)**. *Pick up next two bars on first piece, then next two bars on other **(Figure 3)**. Repeat from * to end of seam, finishing by picking up last bar (or pair of bars) at the top of first piece.

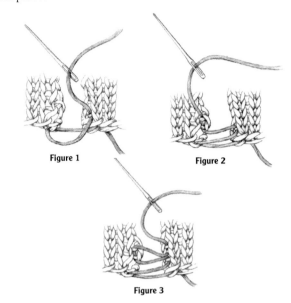

Figure 1   Figure 2

Figure 3

WRAP & TURN (W&T)

Knit row: With yarn in back, slip next st as if to purl, and bring yarn to front **(Figure 1)**. Return the slipped stitch to the left needle **(Figure 2)**. Take the yarn to the back between the needles, and turn the work.

Purl row: With yarn in front, slip next stitch as if to purl, and bring yarn to back. Return the slipped stitch to the left needle, take the yarn to the front between the needles, and turn the work.

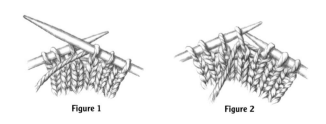

Figure 1   Figure 2

Sources for Yarn

Blue Sky Alpacas/ Spud & Chloë
blueskyalpacas.com

Brooklyn Tweed
brooklyntweed.com

Brown Sheep Company
brownsheep.com

Classic Elite Yarns
classiceliteyarns.com

Claudia Hand Painted Yarns
claudiaco.com

Crafts Americana/KnitPicks
craftsamericana.com

DMC
dmc-usa.com

Fyberspates
fyberspates.co.uk

Lorna's Laces
lornaslaces.net

Madelinetosh
madelinetosh.com

Malabrigo
malabrigoyarn.com

The Natural Dye Studio
thenaturaldyestudio.com

Simply Shetland/ Jamieson's Wools
simplyshetland.net

Skacel/Schoeller Stahl
skacelknitting.com

String Theory
stringtheoryyarn.com

Swans Island
swansislandcompany.com

Tahki-Stacy Charles Inc./ Filatura Di Crosa
tahkistacycharles.com

Westminster Fibers/ Schachenmayr
westminsterfibers.com

Index

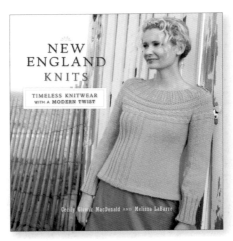
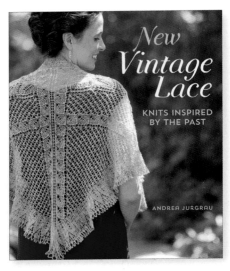
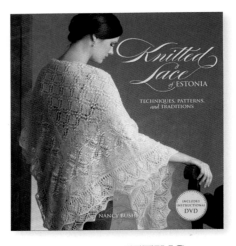